MW01487070

Bash Quick Start Guide

Get up and running with shell scripting with Bash

Tom Ryder

BIRMINGHAM - MUMBAI

Bash Quick Start Guide

Commissioning Editor: Gebin George
Acquisition Editor: Noyonika Das
Content Development Editor: Mohammed Yusuf Imaratwale
Technical Editor: Shweta Jadhav
Copy Editor: Safis Editing
Project Coordinator: Hardik Bhinde
Proofreader: Safis Editing
Indexer: Pratik Shirodkar
Graphics: Jason Monteiro
Production Coordinator: Nilesh Mohite

First published: September 2018

Production reference: 1270918

Published by Packt Publishing Ltd.
Livery Place
35 Livery Street
Birmingham
B3 2PB, UK.

ISBN 978-1-78953-883-0

www.packtpub.com

For Chantelle

– Tom Ryder

`mapt.io`

Mapt is an online digital library that gives you full access to over 5,000 books and videos, as well as industry leading tools to help you plan your personal development and advance your career. For more information, please visit our website.

Why subscribe?

- Spend less time learning and more time coding with practical eBooks and Videos from over 4,000 industry professionals

- Improve your learning with Skill Plans built especially for you

- Get a free eBook or video every month

- Mapt is fully searchable

- Copy and paste, print, and bookmark content

Packt.com

Did you know that Packt offers eBook versions of every book published, with PDF and ePub files available? You can upgrade to the eBook version at `www.packt.com` and as a print book customer, you are entitled to a discount on the eBook copy. Get in touch with us at `customercare@packtpub.com` for more details.

At `www.packt.com`, you can also read a collection of free technical articles, sign up for a range of free newsletters, and receive exclusive discounts and offers on Packt books and eBooks.

Contributors

About the author

Tom Ryder is a systems administrator living in New Zealand who works for an internet services provider. He loves terminals, text editors, network monitoring and security, Unix and GNU/Linux, shell script, and programming in general. He is also the author of the *Nagios Core Administration Cookbook*.

Thanks go to the Packt editors and reviewers; to Richard Stallman, Brian Fox, and Chet Ramey for the GNU Project and the Bourne-Again Shell; to the authors of Greg's Wiki and the Bash Hackers Wiki; to Cory Sadowski for many entertaining chats about shell script over the years; to my boss, James Watts, for contractual permission to write yet another book; and, of course, to the lovely Chantelle Potroz.

About the reviewers

Fabio Alessandro Locati – commonly known as Fale – is the director at Otelia, a public speaker, author, and open source contributor. His primary areas of expertise are Linux, automation, security, and cloud technologies. Fale has more than 14 years' experience working in IT, with many of them spent consulting for companies, including dozens of Fortune 500 companies. Fale has written *Learning Ansible 2*, *OpenStack Cloud Security*, and has been part of the review process for multiple books.

Janos Gyerik is a passionate software developer. He enjoys building software whatever the programming language, both at work and in his spare time. He helps fellow programmers by answering questions on Stack Overflow, or by giving feedback on their code on Code Review Stack Exchange. Janos makes Android apps such as Programming and Bash Quiz, and websites such as Bash One-Liners, and is always up to some geeky projects.

Cory Sadowski is an IT professional living in the United States, specializing in Perl and shell programming, GNU/Linux, and, despite best efforts, Windows administration. He loves most things GNU/Linux, video games, and other such sophisticated topics.

Packt is searching for authors like you

If you're interested in becoming an author for Packt, please visit authors.packtpub.com and apply today. We have worked with thousands of developers and tech professionals, just like you, to help them share their insight with the global tech community. You can make a general application, apply for a specific hot topic that we are recruiting an author for, or submit your own idea.

Table of Contents

Preface

The GNU Bourne-Again Shell, or **Bash**, is the best-known Bourne-style shell in the world, and is installed or available for installation on a huge variety of Unix-like systems. Even professionals who don't do a lot of work with Unix or Linux will need to use the Bash shell occasionally.

Bash is a language of contradictions; while it's the best-known and most widely-deployed shell of its kind, it's perhaps also one of the least-understood tools, with a terse syntax that's relatively unique among modern programming languages and can seem bizarre even to experienced users. Bash is powerful in some ways, and very limited in others. It's clear, elegant, and expressive in some ways, and terse, clumsy, and bewildering in others.

Because it's so powerful and yet so complex, and because so many computer professionals can't avoid using it at least occasionally, Bash is often learned by way of a kind of "tradition;" demonstrations by experienced administrators, reading others' scripts, copying and pasting, and asking questions and reading answers on the internet. This leads to a lot of "cargo-cult programming," and a lot of bad practices that make things unnecessarily confusing at best, and downright dangerous at worst. The available documentation for Bash is often unhelpful in addressing this problem—it often teaches the same bad practices, and even when it's correct, as the official Bash manual page is, it's often too complicated and assumes too much knowledge for new users to understand it.

To avoid all that, we'll start learning good Bash from first principles, and focus almost exclusively on writing the language *well*, in both interactive and batch mode. By the end of this book, you'll have a firm grasp on how to write Bash shell script in a robust and understandable way, and be in a position to notice bad habits and dangerous "hot spots" in others' code. You'll have a great grasp on the problems for which shell script is a perfect solution, and writing it will be a lot more efficient, and maybe even fun.

Who this book is for

This book is ideal for you if you have access to a computer with Bash installed or available, and you've maybe even used Bash or another Unix-like command shell before to enter at least a few basic commands, but you can't understand the official Bash manual page very well (or at all). You should not be ashamed of that; it's one of the most famously dense manual pages for software ever written! Some experience with basic programming structures such as variables, expressions, conditionals, and loops will help you understand the book—but Bash mostly has its own way of doing things that you need to learn from the ground up, so you don't need to be an expert in any given language.

Alternatively, you may be a more experienced systems administrator, or even an expert in another programming language, who has done a fair bit more than a beginner with shell script, but is still frustrated by the dark corners and difficulties in using it, and wants a course in "remedial shell script" to unlearn some bad habits. The book will clarify arcane and difficult syntax and patterns in shell programming. You'll become much more confident in using it in your work when the situation calls for it, and you'll be in a position to fix both your own and others' shell scripts, and even to train others on writing shell script effectively.

What this book covers

Chapter 1, *What is Bash?*, opens the book by giving a clear definition of what the Bash shell actually *is*, where it fits in with other programs on a Unix system, and how to find and (if necessary) install it on your system.

Chapter 2, *Bash Command Structure*, looks at the anatomy of Bash command lines, starting with simple single commands and arguments, and moves on through running multiple commands, and good quoting practices for data.

Chapter 3, *Essential Commands*, examines a list of common commands useful in Bash command lines and scripts, explaining the situations in which each is useful and how to use them; listing, searching, sorting, and slicing data are all discussed.

Chapter 4, *Input, Output, and Redirection*, extends our new basic command structure knowledge to show how to specify where data for commands to read comes from, and where it goes to—including "piping" one command's output into another command, and filtering it in between.

`Chapter` 5, *Variables and Patterns*, explains and demonstrates how Bash's variable assignment and expansion works for both simple variables and arrays, how to transform strings conveniently with parameter expansion, and how to use patterns to match and specify lists of files.

`Chapter` 6, *Loops and Conditionals*, shows how to run the same set of commands on every item of a list of shell words or lines, and how to run commands only if a certain expression is true or false.

`Chapter` 7, *Scripts, Functions, and Aliases*, builds on our new knowledge of shell grammar and common commands to start writing your *own* commands, implemented in the Bash programming language and executable from anywhere on your computer.

`Chapter` 8, *Best Practices*, ends the book with some important hints, tips, and techniques for writing robust and readable shell script that will set you on the path to becoming a true shell scripting expert.

To get the most out of this book

You should have access to a computer with Bash 4.0 or higher installed or available, and be able to type commands into it via a TTY, terminal emulator, Telnet, or SSH connection (for example, using PuTTY). This book does give some guidance in the first chapter on how to install Bash on your system if it's not already there, or if the installed version is too old (as may be the case on macOS X). You will need either administrative-level (`root`) access to the computer to install Bash yourself, or a cooperative systems administrator to help you.

If you are not sure which operating system to use, we recommend the Ubuntu distribution of GNU/Linux, available from `https://www.ubuntu.com/`. The LTS (Long Term Support) version will do fine. Ubuntu is open source, free to download, thoroughly documented, and relatively easy to install. You can run this operating system in a virtual machine using a program or hypervisor such as VMware or VirtualBox—it does not have to be installed directly on your computer's hardware.

At the time of writing, Windows 10 has a new Bash subsystem available and in active development, the Windows Subsystem for Linux. You *may* find that *most* of the material in this book is relevant and usable on such a system, but the book does not specifically support this, and we highly recommend installing a full GNU/Linux or BSD system for your learning and experiments instead.

Download the example code files

You can download the example code files for this book from your account at `www.packt.com`. If you purchased this book elsewhere, you can visit `www.packt.com/support` and register to have the files emailed directly to you.

You can download the code files by following these steps:

1. Log in or register at `www.packt.com`.
2. Select the **SUPPORT** tab.
3. Click on **Code Downloads & Errata**.
4. Enter the name of the book in the **Search** box and follow the onscreen instructions.

Once the file is downloaded, please make sure that you unzip or extract the folder using the latest version of:

- WinRAR/7-Zip for Windows
- Zipeg/iZip/UnRarX for Mac
- 7-Zip/PeaZip for Linux

The code bundle for the book is also hosted on GitHub at `https://github.com/PacktPublishing/Bash-Quick-Start-Guide`. In case there's an update to the code, it will be updated on the existing GitHub repository.

We also have other code bundles from our rich catalog of books and videos available at `https://github.com/PacktPublishing/`. Check them out!

Download the color images

We also provide a PDF file that has color images of the screenshots/diagrams used in this book. You can download it here: `http://www.packtpub.com/sites/default/files/downloads/9781789538830_ColorImages.pdf`.

Conventions used

There are a number of text conventions used throughout this book.

`CodeInText`: Indicates code words in text, database table names, folder names, filenames, file extensions, pathnames, dummy URLs, user input, and Twitter handles. Here is an example: "Mount the downloaded `WebStorm-10*.dmg` disk image file as another disk in your system."

A block of code is set as follows:

```
#!/bin/bash
printf 'Starting script\n' >> log
printf 'Creating test directory\n' >> log
mkdir test || exit
printf 'Changing into test directory\n' >> log
cd test || exit
printf 'Writing current date\n' >> log
date > date || exit
```

Any command-line input or output is written as follows:

```
$ printf 'Hello, world\n' > myfile $ ls -l myfile -rw-r--r-- 1 bashuser
bashuser 1 2018-07-29 20:53:23 myfile
```

Bold: Indicates a new term, an important word, or words that you see onscreen. For example, words in menus or dialog boxes appear in the text like this. Here is an example: "Select **System info** from the **Administration** panel."

Warnings or important notes appear like this.

Tips and tricks appear like this.

Get in touch

Feedback from our readers is always welcome.

General feedback: If you have questions about any aspect of this book, mention the book title in the subject of your message and email us at customercare@packtpub.com.

Errata: Although we have taken every care to ensure the accuracy of our content, mistakes do happen. If you have found a mistake in this book, we would be grateful if you would report this to us. Please visit www.packt.com/submit-errata, selecting your book, clicking on the Errata Submission Form link, and entering the details.

Piracy: If you come across any illegal copies of our works in any form on the Internet, we would be grateful if you would provide us with the location address or website name. Please contact us at copyright@packt.com with a link to the material.

If you are interested in becoming an author: If there is a topic that you have expertise in and you are interested in either writing or contributing to a book, please visit authors.packtpub.com.

Reviews

Please leave a review. Once you have read and used this book, why not leave a review on the site that you purchased it from? Potential readers can then see and use your unbiased opinion to make purchase decisions, we at Packt can understand what you think about our products, and our authors can see your feedback on their book. Thank you!

For more information about Packt, please visit packt.com.

What is Bash? 1

Bash's full name is the GNU **Bourne Again Shell**. It is a programming language, specifically a shell scripting language, with an interpreter in a program named `bash`. It was created by Brian Fox of the Free Software Foundation, starting in 1989, and is now maintained by Chet Ramey. It is part of the GNU project for a free software operating system.

The `bash` program is used as a shell: either for entering commands as an interactive shell using a command line, batches of commands from a shell script, or a single command from an option.

In this book, we will refer to *Bash* as the software distribution and the programming language, and to `bash` as its interpreter program.

Bash is a Bourne-style shell, with some support for POSIX shell compatibility. It is not compatible with any kind of C-style shell, such as `tcsh`.

Bash has many general programming language facilities that make it usable for general programming tasks, but like most shell scripting languages, its fundamental design is to run other programs in a control structure, and to make them work together in ways suitable to the programmer, whether or not they were designed to do so. This is the main thing that makes shell scripting powerful and useful.

In this chapter, you will learn:

- What Bash is and is not
- How to install and switch to Bash
- How to check you are running a recent version of Bash
- How the POSIX standard applies to Bash
- The two major categories of Bash features
- Programming tasks for which Bash is and is not well-suited
- How to get help while using Bash

What Bash is and is not

On reading the preceding definition, you may have noticed a few things you might have expected are missing. There is a lot of confusion out there about what Bash is and is not. Here are some common misconceptions:

- Bash is *not* (necessarily) part of Linux. They are separate pieces of software. GNU Bash existed for several years before the Linux kernel was created, and runs on other operating systems too.
- Bash is *not* the same thing as SSH. SSH is a service and network protocol for running commands on remote computers. `bash` can be one such command.
- Bash is also *not* your terminal or TTY. Your terminal is a device for sending information to, and receiving information from, a computer. Terminals used to be hardware devices with a monitor and keyboard. Nowadays, for most users, they are **terminal emulators**, or software devices. Bash is a program that runs *using* your terminal for its input and output.
- Similarly, Bash is *not* the same thing as PuTTY, iTerm, or xterm. These are terminal emulators, not shells. Your terminal emulator is a program that understands and interprets text-based programs. Bash is one such program.
- Bash is *not* the command line, in the strictest sense. Bash has an interactive mode, which is an example of a command line, but many other tools have command lines, and not just system shells. The `bc` calculator tool is an example of another tool with a command line.

Now that you know this, if someone ever asks you for a PuTTY account on your server, make sure to set them straight!

Getting Bash

If you are running a GNU/Linux system, you almost certainly already have access to Bash. It is installed by default on almost every GNU/Linux computer system.

On such systems, it is very often the default *login shell* for users. This means that when a new user logs in for the first time, it's the first interactive program that runs, and it starts up to wait for command input from the user.

On some systems, such as Debian GNU/Linux, Bash will be the default login shell for non-system users, usually human beings rather than system processes, but a different shell, such as the POSIX shell or Bourne shell, will be used for system accounts.

Bash can be installed on other Unix-like systems as well, such as on FreeBSD, NetBSD, OpenBSD, or proprietary versions of Unix. Even though Bash has such a strong history with GNU/Linux systems, administrators of these other systems often end up installing it, because it is so popular and many users will expect to be able to use it as their shell. It usually has to be installed as a separate package, and is not part of the default installation.

You can also build Bash from source on most Unix-like systems with access to a **C compiler**. Doing this is outside the scope of this book, and you should use your system's packages or ports system if you can. The Bash source code is available at https://www.gnu.org/software/bash/.

Checking Bash is running

If you're using a GNU/Linux system, and your system administrator hasn't changed your login shell, it's likely that Bash is starting up as soon as you log in with a TTY, in an xterm, or over SSH.

If you see a prompt that looks like one of these after you log in, it's a good sign you're in a bash session:

```
bash-4.4$
user@hostname:~$
```

If you want to check, you can enter this at the prompt:

```
bash$ declare -p BASH
```

If you get a response like this, with a path to your bash binary, you can be confident you are running bash:

```
declare -- BASH="/bin/bash"
```

If you get some other output, such as:

```
sh: declare: not found
```

Then you may be running some other kind of shell. You may be able to tell what it is by printing the value of the SHELL variable:

```
$ echo "$SHELL"
```

We'll use the bash$ prefix before commands throughout this book as a way to show commands you should enter at the Bash command line. We'll use just a $ prefix instead if the command should also work in other POSIX-compliant shells.

Switching the login shell to Bash

Even if it's not the shell that starts up when you log in, Bash may still be installed on your system, and you may still be able to change your login shell to it.

You might be able to start it by just typing `bash`:

```
$ bash
```

If you get output like `command not found`, you will probably need to install a Bash package specific to your system, or get your system administrator to do it for you. Consult your operating system's documentation to learn how to do this.

If you get a new prompt that looks like the Bash prompts in the previous section, you can then find the location of the `bash` program:

```
bash$ declare -p BASH
BASH="/usr/local/bin/bash"
```

Depending on the system, you might then be able to change Bash to your login shell to that path with the `chsh` tool:

```
$ chsh -s /usr/local/bin/bash
```

This might prompt you for your system password to allow you to make the change.

You may get an error message like this:

```
chsh: /usr/local/bin/bash is an invalid shell
```

In this case, the `invalid shell` part likely means that the path given needs to be added to the `/etc/shells` file, which specifies the programs the system and its administrator have allowed as login shells. You can inspect this list with `cat`:

```
$ cat /etc/shells
```

If you add your full path to `bash` on your system to that file, the `chsh` call should then succeed.

Identifying the Bash version number

Before we start writing commands and programming with Bash, it's a good idea to find out what version of Bash you have installed. This is because newer versions of Bash have useful new features that might be discussed in this book, but that might not be available in your version of Bash.

You can check the version of your current running shell by printing the value of the BASH_VERSION variable:

```
bash$ declare -p BASH_VERSION
declare -- BASH_VERSION="4.4.12(1)-release"
```

You can get the same information by invoking the bash program with its --version option, which provides some extra information about the program's version number and software license:

```
$ bash --version
GNU bash, version 4.4.12(1)-release (x86_64-pc-linux-gnu)
Copyright (C) 2016 Free Software Foundation, Inc.
License GPLv3+: GNU GPL version 3 or later
<http://gnu.org/licenses/gpl.html>

This is free software; you are free to change and redistribute it.
There is NO WARRANTY, to the extent permitted by law.
```

The most recent stable *minor* version of GNU Bash at the time of writing is version 4.4, with version 4.4.0 released in September 2016.

In this book, we will focus on the features of Bash that were available in GNU Bash version 4.0, which was released in 2011, and is very widely available as a minimum version.

If the version of Bash installed on your computer is older than 4.0, some of the scripts and features discussed in this book may not work correctly. You or your system administrator should use your operating system to upgrade your Bash shell to a newer version.

Upgrading Bash on macOS X

There is a special case of Bash versions for macOS X. If you are using Bash on OS X, you might notice that the version of Bash installed by default is much older than the minimum of 4.0 discussed in this book:

```
bash$ declare -p BASH_VERSION
declare -- BASH_VERSION="3.2.57(1)-release"
```

This is due to licensing changes in Bash 4.0 that were not acceptable to the operating system vendor, which leaves the version of Bash included on the system stuck at the last acceptable version. This means that, by default, your system may not have Bash 4.0 or newer, even if the system is brand new.

Fortunately, there are other ways to install Bash 4.0 or newer on a macOS X computer. One popular method is to use the Homebrew package-management system, available here: http://brew.sh/.

Follow the instructions on the Homebrew website to install it. You can then install a new version of Bash with:

```
$ brew install bash
```

You may have to include the newly-installed Bash path in the allowed list of login shells in /etc/shells before you can apply chsh to change your login shell. You may also have to adjust your terminal emulator (e.g. iTerm) to run the new version of Bash. Consult your operating system and terminal emulator documentation to learn how to do this.

Understanding Bash features

Some of Bash's programming features are shared by all other Bourne-style, POSIX-compatible Shell scripting languages. These are specified by the POSIX standard, in section 2, *Shell Command Language*. Bash is designed to conform to this standard. You can read what it specifies at http://pubs.opengroup.org/onlinepubs/9699919799/utilities/V3_chap02.html.

Bash also has many other features that are not described in the POSIX shell script standard that make many common shell script programming tasks easier. In this book, we will examine both categories.

POSIX shell script features

Features required for the POSIX shell script include:

- **Running commands** convenient syntax for **running commands**, including other programs, specifying arguments, environment variables, working directories, permissions masking, and other properties.

- **Variables** that can be set to any string value, including manipulating process environment variables, and that can be expanded on the command line.

- **Arithmetic expansion** for performing integer-based arithmetic on variables and numbers.

- **Control structures** for executing code depending on the outcome of another command (`if`), including a specially-designed `test` or `[` command, and repeating code until a condition is true (`while`).

- **Aliases** as a way to abbreviate long command lines as a single word for convenience.

- **Functions** to allow defining blocks of code as new commands for the purposes of the running script or interactive session.

- **Input and output redirection** to specify input sources and output destinations for programs run in the shell.

- **Pipes** to direct the output of one command to become the input of another.

- **Argument list** through which code can iterate using a `for` loop.

- **Parameter expansion** a means of switching between or transforming string values in assignments or command arguments.

- **Pattern matching** in the form of classic Unix **globs**.

- **Process management** in running jobs in the background, and waiting for them to complete at the desired point.

- **Compound commands** to treat a group of commands as one, optionally running it in a **subshell environment** (subprocess).

- **Reading lines of input data** including breaking them down into fields with a defined separator character.

- **Formatted strings** such as the C `printf(3)` function in the `stdio` C programming language library.

- **Command substitution** to use the output of a command as a variable, as part of a test, or as an argument to another command.

These features are either part of the Shell scripting language itself, or available in the POSIX-specified programs that it calls. In a sense, your shell scripts are only limited by the programs you can run with them.

By calling the `grep` program, for example, you can select input lines using **regular expressions**, even if your Shell scripting language does not itself support regular expressions. We will cover some of these essential commands in this book, even though they are not technically part of the GNU Bash distribution.

All the these features mean you can get a lot done in your Bash program even if you just use POSIX features, and your script might then run on other shells, such as `dash`, without much modification. All of the features are discussed in this book.

Bash-specific features

In addition to all the POSIX shell script features in the previous section, Bash adds many extensions that make programming more convenient, expressive, and sometimes less error-prone. These include:

- Named **array** variables. This is perhaps the most important advantage over the plain POSIX shell script. It makes many otherwise impractical things possible. If you need one single reason to use Bash, this is probably it!
- An easier syntax for performing conditional tests. This is also a very important feature.
- **Extended globs** for advanced pattern-matching.
- **Regular expression** support, for performing the most powerful kind of text-pattern-matching, when even globs won't do.
- **Local variables** for functions, a limited kind of variable scope.
- A **C-style** `for` **loop syntax.**
- Several kinds of **parameter expansion**, including case transformation, array slices, substrings, substitution, and quoting.
- Arithmetic expressions, for conveniently testing the outcome of arithmetic operations.
- Many more shell options to control shell script and interactive shell behavior, including extra debugging support.
- Better support for **irregular filenames** and **unusual line separators** in data.

All of these features are also discussed in this book. Where relevant, we will specify which features are POSIX-specific and which features are specific to Bash.

Do I need Bash?

If you know you will have Bash available on the systems where your shell script will run, you should use it! Its features make programming in shell script easier and safer, and it is by far the most popular kind of shell script, with many people reading and writing it. Many people think that Bash is the *only* kind of shell script.

Even if your shell script is simple today, you might need to add more to it tomorrow, and a Bash feature might be exactly the thing you need at that time.

However, if your shell script might need to run on a system where Bash may not be installed and cannot be installed for your script, then you may need to limit yourself to the POSIX shell features. Check your system's documentation to determine what style of shell script you will have to write in order for your script to run.

Choosing when to apply Bash

There are some tasks for which shell scripting in general, and Bash in particular, are especially well-suited:

- **Prototyping**: Short Bash programs are quick and easy to write. It's quite common to "hack together" a simple script in Bash for later replacement by a script or program in a more advanced programming language that requires more effort to write and maintain.

- **Interactive system administration**: A Bourne-style shell is assumed in very many contexts in Unix, and almost all of the system documentation you read will tell you to issue commands in a Bourne-style shell. This makes it a natural choice for a scripting language.

- **Automation**: If you have a set of commands you often run together, making a script for them is as simple as writing them all into a text file, each on a new line, and making that file executable.

- **Connecting programs together**: Like all Shell scripting languages, Bash specializes in moving data to and from files and between processes. Many programs are designed to work together in this way.

- **Filtering and transforming text input**: Some programs, however, *aren't* designed to cooperate in this way, and they require some data **filtering and transformation** in the middle. Bash can be a very convenient language for doing this, and it's also a good language to call other tools such as `awk` or `sed` to do it for you.

- **Navigating the Unix filesystem**: In Bash, it does not require much code to navigate and iterate through the filesystem, discovering, filtering, and processing files within it at runtime. Coupled with the `find` tool, especially a high-powered version such as GNU `find`, a lot can be done in a pattern over a filesystem with relatively little code.

- **Basic pattern-matching on strings**: Bash has features that make it good for basic pattern-matching on strings, especially filenames and path names, with **parameter expansion**.

- **Portability**: Bash works on and is packaged for a huge variety of Unix-like systems. POSIX shell script is even more widely supported. If you need to know your script and its runtime will remain portable to many Unix-like systems, Bash might be a good choice.

Choosing when to avoid Bash

Bash's design and development effort is less focussed on some other areas. New users who are keen to use Bash often find tasks that require the following to be difficult or impossible in the Bash language itself:

- **Programs requiring speed**: The end of the Bash manual page, under the "BUGS" section, reads: *It's too big and too slow*. This may seem like a joke, but while a compiled `bash` binary is unlikely to be more than a couple of megabytes in size, it is not optimized for speed. Depending on the task, reading a very large file line by line in Bash and processing data within it with string operations is likely to be significantly slower than using a tool such as `sed` or `awk`.

- **Fixed or floating-point math**: Bash has no built-in support for fixed or floating-point mathematical operations. It can call programs such as `awk` or `bc` to do such things on its behalf, but if you need to do a lot of this, you might want to just write the whole program in AWK, or maybe in Perl instead.

- **Long or complex programs**: The ideal Bash program is short and sweet – less than 100 lines of code is ideal. Bash programs much longer than this can rapidly become unmanageable. This is partly a consequence of the terse syntax, and partly because the complexity of a script increases faster when much of the work is invoking *other* programs, as shell scripts tend to do.

- **Serialization**: Bash has no native support for serialized data formats such as JSON, XML, or YAML. Again, this is best delegated to third-party tools such as `jq` or `xmlstar`, which Bash can call from within scripts. Trying to do this in just Bash is an exercise in frustration for newer programmers.

- **Network programming**: Bash does have some support for network programming on some systems, but it does not allow much fine-grained control. It mostly has to lean on external tools such as `netcat` or `curl` to do this.

- **Object-oriented programming**: Object-oriented programming is not practical in Bash. It does not have any concept of a namespace or classes, a system of modules to separate code, nor any object system.

- **Functional programming**: Bash's language design means it does not have any of the primitives that users of functional languages, such as Lisp, Scheme, or Haskell, might expect from a language. It has very limited support for lexical scope, read-only data, indirection (references), or data structures more complex than arrays. It has no support for closures or related features.

- **Concurrent programming**: Bash *generally* just runs commands in sequence. It's possible to run processes in parallel, and to simulate basic concurrency concepts such as locks, but a programming language built with concurrency in mind may be a better choice for tasks requiring multithreading or parallel processing.

Getting help with Bash

Sometimes in technical books, people skip the *Getting help* heading. **Don't skip this one!** It's very important, and will save you a lot of time and confusion.

You can get help on using most of the commands in this book with a two-step process. When you're using Bash, to get help on a command named `printf`, use `help` first:

```
bash$ help printf
```

You'll get some help output, so you now know that `printf` is a Bash keyword or builtin. That's the version of the command you want help with, because that's the one that you'll be using when you call it from within Bash.

To see why this is confusing, try the `man` manual reader command, instead:

```
bash$ man printf
```

You'll get a completely different document, a full manual page! The features aren't even the same! What's going on?

In a shell script, the same command can have more than one implementation. In Bash, you can see a list of all of them using the `type` command with its `-a` (all) switch:

```
bash$ type -a printf
printf is a shell builtin
printf is /usr/bin/printf
```

Notice how there are *two* results for `printf`: the first is a shell builtin – a part of Bash itself – and the second is a program on your filesystem. They will behave differently and have different documentation. We'll see more of the `type` command in later chapters.

So remember: *always* try `help` first! Some people use Bash for many years before learning it exists, and wonder why the `man` pages are always wrong. You can see a full list of available `help` topics by typing it on its own, with no arguments:

```
bash$ help
```

Summary

Effective Bash programming begins with a good understanding of what Bash actually is, and how it fits into your system. It's useful to know which features are in Bash because they implement the POSIX standard for shell scripting, and which features are specific to Bash, especially because it will help you decide on the portability of your shell script. It's also very relevant for deciding whether Bash is the right tool for any given job.

Bash Command Structure

2

In this chapter, we'll learn the structure of a simple Bash command line, and the basics of quoting. You should read this chapter all the way through, paying careful attention especially to the material on quoting, even if you feel you already know how Bash commands work.

In this chapter, you will learn the following:

- How to use Bash interactively
- The structure of simple commands
- How to quote data safely
- How to run several commands with one command line
- How to make a command line stop if a command fails
- How to run a command in the background

Using Bash interactively

If Bash is your login shell, and you log in to the system from a terminal or terminal emulator, then it will start in interactive mode. In this mode, Bash will present a prompt when it's ready to accept a command from your terminal. This differs from non-interactive or batch mode, where commands are read from some other source, such as a script file. We will use interactive mode in this chapter to experiment with the basics of shell script command line grammar.

Nearly all of the features available to Bash in scripts are also available on the interactive command line, and they behave essentially the same way as if you ran them from a script. This allows you to treat the interactive command line as a live scripting environment: you can assign variables, create functions, and manage control flow and processes.

Interactive key bindings

In this book, we won't focus too much on the interactive keyboard shortcuts in Bash. This is because it's more useful to know the syntax of the shell scripting language than it is to know key bindings.

To read more about Bash key bindings, after you have finished this book, consult the Bash manual under the *READLINE* section, and the GNU Readline manual:

```
$ man bash
$ man 3 readline
```

Simple commands

At an interactive Bash prompt, you can enter a command line for Bash to execute. Most often while in interactive mode, you would issue only one simple command at a time, ending each command with Enter. You would then wait for each command to finish before entering the next one, examining any output or errors that it passes to your terminal after each command.

A simple command consists of at least a command name, possibly with one or more arguments, each separated by at least one space. The full definition can also include environment variable assignments and redirection operators, which we'll explore in later chapters.

Let's consider the following command:

```
$ mkdir -p New/bash
```

This simple command consists of three shell words:

- mkdir: The command name, referring to the mkdir program that creates a directory
- -p: An option string for mkdir that specifies that the full directory path can be created, whether or not any of the directories in the path already exist
- New/bash: The relative path for the directory to create

Note that -p is not a special word or syntax to Bash; it's special to mkdir. Bash simply passes it to mkdir as an argument. The meaning of command options is a property of the commands themselves, not the shell from which they're called.

Shell metacharacters

So far, all of our examples of commands and arguments have been single unquoted shell words. However, there is a set of **metacharacters** that have a different meaning to Bash, and trying to use them as part of a word causes problems.

For example, suppose you want to create (touch) a new file named important file. Note that there's a space in the name. If you try to create it as follows, you get unexpected results:

```
$ touch important file
```

If we list the files in the directory after running this, using ls -1 to put all the names on separate lines, we can see we've actually created *two* files; one named important, and one named file:

```
$ ls -1
file
important
```

This happened because the space between the two words separated them into two separate arguments. Space, tab, and newline are all metacharacters. So are | (pipe), & (ampersand), ; (semicolon), (and) (parentheses), and < and > (angle brackets).

There are many other characters interpreted specially by Bash in some contexts, including {, [, *, and $, but these are not considered metacharacters according to the manual page's definition.

Even the error messages can be confusing if you try to use a word with one of these characters in it:

```
$ touch Testfile<Tom>.doc
bash: Tom: No such file or directory

$ touch Review;Final.doc
bash: Final.doc: command not found
```

In some cases, you may not get an error message at all, and something very unexpected will happen instead; for example:

```
$ touch $$$Money.doc
$ ls
31649.doc
```

A lot of the time we can simply work with files and words that don't use these characters. However, we can't always do that, and we can't just hope others behave the same way—we will eventually have to work with their files and data. How can we include special characters in our words safely?

Quoting

The way you can reliably include characters that are special to Bash *literally* in a command line is to *quote* them. Quoting special characters makes Bash ignore any special meaning they may otherwise have to the shell, and instead use them as plain characters, like a-z or 0-9. This works for *almost* any special character.

We say "almost", because there's one exception: there's no way to escape the null character (ASCII NUL, 0x00) in a shell word.

Quoting is the *most important thing* that even experienced people who write shell script sometimes get wrong. Even a lot of very popular documentation online fails to quote correctly in example scripts! If you learn to quote correctly, you will save yourself a lot of trouble down the line. The way quoting in shell script works very often surprises people coming from other programming languages.

We will look at three kinds of quoting: escaping, single-quoting, and double-quoting.

Escaping

Using escaping with *backslashes*, the examples from the previous section can be correctly written like this:

```
$ touch important\ files
$ touch Testfile\<Tom\>.doc
$ touch Review\;Final.doc
$ touch \$\$\$Money.doc
```

A backslash can escape another backslash, too:

```
$ echo \\backslash\\
\backslash\
```

However, it can't escape a newline within a word:

```
$ echo backslash\
> foo\
> bar
backslashfoobar
```

Single quotes

Using *single quotes*, we could write the commands like this, which is perhaps more readable than the backslashes version, and creates files with identical names:

```
$ touch 'important files'
$ touch 'Testfile<Tom>.doc'
$ touch 'Review;Final.doc'
$ touch '$$$Money.doc'
```

Unlike backslashes, single quotes *can* escape a newline in a word:

```
$ echo 'quotes
> foo
> bar'
quotes
foo
bar
```

How do we use a single quote (') as a literal character between two single quotes? If you are coming to Bash from a language such as Perl or PHP, you might try it like this, with a backslash, but that doesn't work:

```
$ echo 'It\'s today'
>
```

This is because backslash is *not* treated specially within single quotes. Doubling the single quote doesn't work, either:

```
$ echo 'It''s today'
Its today
```

In this case, Bash just sees two single-quoted strings, It and s today, and pushes them together as one word. The way to do it is to use a backslash *outside* of the single quotes:

```
$ echo 'It'\''s today'
It's today
```

Double quotes

Double quotes behave similarly to single quotes, but they perform certain kinds of *expansion* within them, for shell variables and substitutions. This can be used to include the value of a variable as part of a literal string:

```
$ echo "This is my login shell: $SHELL"
This is my login shell: /bin/bash
```

Compare this to the literal output of single quotes:

```
$ echo 'This is my login shell: $SHELL'
This is my login shell: $SHELL
```

Other kinds of parameter expansion within double quotes are possible, which we will examine in later chapters.

You can include a literal dollar sign or backslash in a string by escaping it:

```
$ echo "Not a variable: \$total"
Not a variable: $total
$ echo "Back\\to\\back\\slashes"
Back\to\back\slashes
```

Exclamation marks are a special case, due to **history expansion**; you will generally need to quote them with a backslash or single quotes instead of double quotes:

```
$ echo "Hello $USER"'!!'
Hello bashuser!!
```

For historical reasons, you will also need to escape *backtick* characters (`):

```
$ echo "Backticks: \`\`\`"
Backticks:  ```
```

Quote concatenation

You may have noticed from the examples in the previous section that you can put different types of quoting together in the same word, as long as they can never separated by an unquoted space:

```
$ echo Hello,\ "$USER"'! Welcome to '"$HOSTNAME"'!'
Hello, bashuser! Welcome to bashdemo!
```

In Bash, there's no concatenation operator like Perl or PHP's dot (.); to concatenate strings, you just put them next to each other. This can be a good idea if you have a mix of literal strings and variables in a single shell word, as it can help you avoid getting caught out by a stray dollar sign, backtick, exclamation mark, or backslash within double-quote pairs.

Running commands in sequence

You can send an interactive command line with *more than one* simple command in it, separating them with a *semicolon*, one of several possible **control operators**. Bash will then execute the commands in sequence, waiting for each simple command to finish before it starts the next one. For example, we could write the following command line and issue it in an interactive Bash session:

```
$ cd ; ls -a ; mkdir New
```

Running `cd` on its own like this, with no directory target argument, is a shortcut to take you to your home directory. It's the same as typing `cd ~` or `cd -- "$HOME"`.

For this command line, note that even if one of the commands fails, Bash will still keep running the next command. To demonstrate this, we can write a command line to include a command that we expect to fail, such as the `rmdir` call here:

```
$ cd ; rmdir ~/nonexistent ; echo 'Hello'
rmdir: failed to remove '/home/bashuser/nonexistent': No such file or
directory
Hello
```

Note that the `echo` command still runs, even though the `rmdir` command before it did not succeed. If you want your set of commands to stop if one of them fails, separating them with semicolons is the wrong choice.

Exit values

We can tell it was the `rmdir` command in the previous section that failed, because `rmdir` is the first word of the error message output. We can test the command in isolation, and look at the value of the special `$?` parameter with `echo`, to see its **exit status**:

```
$ rmdir ~/nonexistent
rmdir: failed to remove '/home/bashuser/nonexistent': No such file or
```

```
directory
$ echo $?
1
```

The `rmdir` program returned an exit value of `1`, because it could not delete a directory that didn't exist. If we create a directory first, and then remove it, both commands succeed, and the value of `$?` for both steps is `0`:

```
$ mkdir ~/existent
$ echo $?
0
$ rmdir ~/existent
$ echo $?
0
```

Examining the exit values for the `true` and `false` built-in Bash commands is instructive; `true` always succeeds, and `false` always fails:

```
$ true ; echo $?
0
$ false ; echo $?
1
```

Bash will also raise an exit status of `127` for you if it can't find a way to run a command you request, such as `notacommand`:

```
$ notacommand ; echo $?
bash: notacommand: command not found
127
```

It's standard for programs to return 0 when they *succeed*, and something greater than 0 if they *fail*. Beyond that, programs vary in which exit values they choose for error conditions.

Stopping a command list on error

Most of the time when programming in Bash, you will not actually want to test `$?` directly, but instead test it implicitly as *success* or *failure*, with language features in Bash itself.

If you wanted to issue a set of commands on one command line, but only to continue if every command worked, you would use the double-ampersand (`&&`) control operator, instead of the semicolon (`;`):

```
$ cd && rmdir ~/nonexistent && ls
```

When we run this command line, we see that the final `ls` never runs, because the `rmdir` command before it failed:

```
rmdir: failed to remove '/home/user/nonexistent': No such file or directory
```

Similarly, if we changed the `cd` command at the start of the command line to change into a directory that didn't exist, the command line would stop even earlier:

```
bash$ cd ~/nonexistent && rmdir ~/nonexistent && ls
bash: cd: /home/bashuser/nonexistent: No such file or directory
```

In `Chapter 6`, *Loops and Conditionals*, we'll explore more fully Bash's options for *control flow*, including using the `||` command separator, and using the `if` command to execute blocks of code conditional on a test outcome.

Running a command in the background

There are some situations in which you might want to continue running other commands as you wait for another one to complete, to run more than one job in *parallel*. You can arrange for a command to run in the background by ending it with a single ampersand (`&`) control operator.

You can try this out by issuing a `sleep` command in the background. The `sleep` built-in Bash command accepts a number of seconds to wait as an argument. If you enter such a command without the `&`, Bash won't accept further commands until the command exits:

```
$ sleep 10
# Ten seconds pass...
$
```

However, if you add the `&` terminator to start the job in the background, the behavior is different: you get a job control number and a process ID, and you are returned immediately to your prompt:

```
$ sleep 10 &
[1] 435
$
```

You can continue running other commands as normal while this job is running in the background. After the 10 seconds are up, the next time the prompt appears, it will also print output telling you the job has completed:

```
[1]+  Done                    sleep 10
$
```

Summary

Even if you feel that you already know the basic structure of a Bash command well, carefully looking at the structure of a typical command line and knowing the rules of string quoting can make it much clearer what's wrong when something doesn't behave as expected. We use single quotes to keep characters literal, and double quotes to safely perform expansion for variables and substitutions. Developing disciplined habits with quoting and understanding how Bash runs commands in sequence is helpful not just for scripting, but for interactive command line work as well.

Having learned the structure of a Bash command line, in the next chapter we'll apply it to learning some essential commands that will form the basis of many shell scripts.

3
Essential Commands

In this chapter, we'll be going through some of the commands essential for good Bash scripting. Bash programming, and shell script programming in general, is different from most other programming languages because it is designed to run *other* programs, mixing the commands it provides with commands installed on the local system.

It may seem strange that in a Bash book, we would spend half a chapter explaining how to use commands that are neither part of Bash, nor written in the Bash language! The reason we do this is that most useful Bash scripts will use several of these external commands to do their work, particularly to do things that in the Bash language are difficult, awkward, or even impossible.

Distinguishing command types

The commands you can use in a Bash script fall into three major categories:

- **Shell builtin commands**: Included in Bash itself. These commands don't correspond to executable program files on your system; they are implemented in the `bash` binary itself. Examples are `echo`, `type`, and `source`.
- **Runtime commands**: Defined in the shell at runtime, and written in the Bash language. These can be aliases or functions. They don't have executable program files of their own on disk either, and are defined at runtime during a Bash session, often by reading startup files. Examples vary between systems and users.
- **System commands**: Invoke executable program files on your filesystem. These are the only kinds of commands that can also be run *outside* of Bash. Examples are `grep`, `ping`, and `rm`.

The executable programs called by system commands may be written in any language. Bash can be used to specify how these programs run, where their input comes from, how their output is processed, and how their success or failure changes the execution of the rest of the script.

We will explore useful commands in the first and third categories in this chapter. Runtime commands (aliases and functions) are discussed in `Chapter 7`, *Scripts, Functions, and Aliases*. In this chapter, you will learn how to use these essential builtin commands:

- `type`: Finding what a command is
- `echo`: Printing arguments
- `printf`: Printing formatted arguments
- `pwd`: Printing the current directory
- `cd`: Changing the current directory
- `set`: Viewing and setting shell properties
- `declare`: Managing variables and functions
- `test`, `[`, `[[`: Evaluating expressions

You will also learn how to use these system commands, which are not part of Bash itself:

- `ls`: Listing files for users
- `mv`: Moving and renaming files
- `cp`: Copying files
- `rm` and `rmdir`: Deleting files and directories
- `grep`: Matching patterns
- `cut`: Extracting columns from data
- `wc`: Counting lines, words, and characters
- `find`: Iterating through a file tree
- `sort` and `uniq`: Sorting and de-duplicating input

 We will not be covering the use of interactive text editors, such as `emacs`, `nano`, and `vi`, due to space concerns. It's a very good idea for an aspiring Bash programmer to learn how to use one of those editors, however! Your author recommends `vi`, especially the Vim implementation.

Essential Bash builtin commands

The first category of essential commands that we'll examine are builtins: they are included as part of the `bash` program. In fact, the very first command we'll look at, called `type`, is itself designed to help you tell what any kind of command is.

For all of these commands, Bash can provide help on usage with the `help` program. For example, to get help on the `type` command, you would type:

```
bash$ help type
```

The type command

The `type` command, given the name of any command or commands, gives you information about what kind of command it is:

```
bash$ type echo
echo is a shell builtin
bash$ type grep
grep is /bin/grep
```

It identifies shell *keyword*, too:

```
bash$ type for
for is a shell keyword
```

We can define a function and an alias to test that it correctly detects those:

```
bash$ myfunc() { : ; }
bash$ type myfunc
myfunc is a function
myfunc ()
{
    :
}
bash$ alias myalias=:
bash$ type myalias
myalias is aliased to `:'
```

The `type` command has a few useful options. If you use the `-t` option, you can get a single word specifying the command type. This is sometimes useful in scripts:

```
bash$ type -t echo
builtin
bash$ type -t grep
file
```

If you use the −a option, you can see *all* commands that have the same name. Bash will print them in order of preference. For example, the true name probably has both a builtin command and a system command on your system:

```
bash$ type -a true
true is a shell builtin
true is /bin/true
```

Bash will always prefer builtin commands for a given name over system commands. If you want to call the system's implementation of true, you could do it by specifying the full path to the program:

```
$ /bin/true
```

 Try type −a [and then type −a [[. Are you surprised by any of the output?

Another useful switch for type is −P, which will look for a system command for the given name, and print out the path to it if found:

```
bash$ type -P true
/bin/true
```

Note that the /bin/true path was returned, even though true is also the name of a shell builtin.

There is a reason we put the type command first in this list. After help, it is the most useful Bash command for understanding the language, and clearing up the biggest source of confusion about the language: *When I run this command, what is actually running?*

The echo command

The echo builtin command just repeats the arguments you provide it onto the standard output:

```
$ echo Hello
Hello
```

This makes it a simple way to emit content to the terminal, including variables:

```
$ echo 'Hello, '"$USER"\!
Hello, bashuser!
```

The `echo` command in Bash has switches that allow you to control the output, such as excluding the final newline, or expanding sequences such as `\t` to tab characters. However, we caution against using `echo` in scripts, because for historical reasons it has broken design and portability problems that makes it confusing or error-prone to use, especially when trying to use it with switches. We suggest you always use `printf` in scripts instead, as its behavior is more predictable, especially when printing variables or control characters such as newlines.

The printf command

The `printf` command works like `echo`, except the first argument you provide to it is a *format string*:

```
$ printf '%s\n' 'Hello!'
Hello!
```

Notice that we had to put the format string in single quotes, to prevent the backslash from having special meaning to the shell. Notice also that we didn't have to use double quotes to get the newline from `\n`; the `printf` command did that for us.

You can use `printf` in much the same way you would use a `printf()` function in other languages, such as C. It supports most of the same format specifications as the `printf(1)` system command; you can type `man 1 printf` to see a list.

It's easier to print tricky strings with `printf`, where `echo` might struggle:

```
$ printf '%s\n' -n
-n
$ string=-n
$ printf '%s\n' "$string"
-n
```

You should always choose `printf` over `echo` in scripts, even though it's a little more typing.

Be careful with what you put into a format string; a variable with a value provided by the user can be a security hole! It's best to use only fixed format strings, or carefully build them yourself.

`printf` also has a useful property where it will repeat the format string as necessary for each argument you provide it. This is a convenient way to print a list of arguments on individual lines:

```
$ printf '%s\n' foo bar baz
foo
bar
baz
```

Note that we got three instances of the string-newline pattern from one format string.

Finally, Bash's `printf` has a `%q` pattern that can be used to quote special characters in a string with backslashes, so it can be reused safely in the shell. If you follow good quoting practices, you are unlikely to need this a lot in Bash, but it's useful to know it's there:

```
bash$ printf '%q\n' 'Watch out for thi$ $tring; it \has\ nasty character$!'
Watch\ out\ for\ thi\$\ \$tring\;\ it\ \\has\\\ nasty\ character\$\!
```

The pwd command

The `pwd` Bash builtin prints the current *working directory* for the script to the standard output:

```
$ pwd
/home/bashuser
```

 This information is also available in the `PWD` environment variable, which can be more flexible to use in scripts.

The working directory for the shell refers to the directory from which all *relative paths* are based, even if they have multiple levels of directories in them:

```
$ pwd
/home/bashuser/docs
$ ls important/doc1.txt
important/doc1.txt
$ ls doc2.txt
doc2.txt
$ ls nonexistent
ls: cannot access 'nonexistent': No such file or directory
```

Any path that *starts* with a forward slash – a *leading slash* – is instead an *absolute path*, and resolves independently of the current directory:

```
$ ls /home/bashuser/important/doc1.txt
/home/bashuser/important/doc1.txt
$ ls /home/bashuser/doc2.txt
/home/bashuser/doc2.txt
```

Tilde paths

A path that starts with a *tilde* character (~) is interpreted specially by the shell, for *tilde expansion* into a system user's home directory. By itself, it refers to the current user's home directory:

```
$ echo ~
/home/bashuser
$ echo ~/important
/home/bashuser/important
```

In this circumstance, it checks the value of the HOME environment variable first if it can. However, if this variable is blank or if the tilde is followed by any valid system username, Bash will attempt to find the home directory for that user with reference to the system password file, usually /etc/passwd:

```
$ echo ~root
/root
$ echo ~root/.ssh
/root/.ssh
```

If the user does not exist, Bash will leave the tilde string the same, without raising an error:

```
$ echo ~notauser
~notauser
```

If you want to print a tilde for a real user *without* expanding it, you need to quote it. Escaping, single-quoting, and double-quoting all work:

```
$ echo ~bashuser
/home/bashuser
$ echo \~bashuser '~bashuser' "~bashuser"
~bashuser ~bashuser ~bashuser
```

The cd command

Where `pwd` or `$PWD` *gets* the current working directory for the shell, the `cd` Bash builtin command *sets* the working directory:

```
$ pwd
/home/bashuser
$ cd /tmp
$ pwd
/tmp
```

When issued with no arguments, the `cd` command defaults to the current user's home directory. Again, it does this by reading the `$HOME` environment variable first, if it can:

```
$ cd
$ pwd
/home/bashuser
```

You can change to the *parent* of the current directory with the `. .` name:

```
$ pwd
/home/bashuser
$ cd ..
$ pwd
/home
```

Changing the directory in scripts

The `cd` builtin works both interactively or as part of a script; in fact, you can change the directory inside of a script run from Bash, and it will not change your running shell. Suppose we had a script in the `lstemp.bash` file with the following two commands:

```
cd /tmp
ls
```

We can run that script from any directory, and even though part of the script is to change the directory to `/tmp`, we won't be left there:

```
$ pwd
/home/bashuser/scripts
$ ls
lstemp.bash
$ bash lstemp.bash
tmpfile1 tmpfile2 tmpfile3
$ pwd
/home/bashuser/scripts
```

This is because the script runs as its own *subprocess*, and hence has its own working directory that can be changed without affecting any other process. We'll learn more about this in the material on subprocesses and *subshells* in Chapter 7, *Scripts, Functions, and Aliases*.

There's also an important note about using cd safely in scripts in Chapter 8, *Best Practices*.

The set command

The set builtin command is one of the most misunderstood (and overloaded!) commands in Bash. It does several different things depending on how it's called: show names, set shell options, and set shell positional parameters.

First of all, when run on its own with no arguments, set prints a list of all of the variables and any functions for the running shell, in alphabetical order. It includes the full definition of the functions. This is one of several ways to view all of the variables in the shell. We suggest you use declare instead, explained later in this chapter, as it shows more information about properties of the variables.

Secondly, set allows you to specify certain options for how the shell runs, all options starting with a single dash, –. The complete list of the options that can be set is too long to explain here, but is available in help set. Some options of note:

- –e: Exit immediately if a command exits with a non-zero status. This is used in scripts as a way to stop running the script if anything goes wrong. Because this option's behavior can be hard to predict, it's generally better to write your own error-handling for all but the most simple scripts.

- –n: Read commands but don't execute them. This is a useful way to check that your Bash script is syntactically correct without actually running any of the commands. Note that this is not perfect, however; some subtle properties of the Bash syntax can change during a script run, and the –n option might not catch that.

- –v: Print shell input lines as they are read. This can be good for debugging, but does not show as much information as –x.

- –x: Print commands and their arguments as they are executed. Turning this option on is often a very good first step for debugging a Bash script, as it shows you how the bash program has interpreted and expanded its input.

These options work the same way as if you had started the `bash` program with that option; for example, `set -x` in the shell has the same effect as starting the shell as `bash -x`, or having a script's *shebang* line include the option, such as `#!/bin/bash -x`.

Finally, `set` followed by the option terminator string, `--`, can be used to set the *positional parameters* for the shell. We will examine these special parameters in more detail in Chapter 6, *Loops and Conditionals*.

The declare command

The `declare` builtin sets or displays variables (including arrays) and functions. It's not usually needed for setting variables, but it's a good way to get an overview of your shell's current running state, providing more information than the `set` builtin.

Run with only the `-p` option, `declare` prints the values of all of the variables in the current shell environment, along with some short option flags that describe their properties:

```
bash$ declare -p
declare -- BASH="/bin/bash"
declare -r BASHOPTS="cdspell:checkhash:checkjobs:checkwinsize:..."
declare -ir BASHPID
declare -A BASH_ALIASES=()
declare -a BASH_ARGC=()
...
```

If you include the names of any variables after `-p`, *without* the dollar sign prefix, Bash will print results only for those names:

```
bash$ declare -p BASH PWD
declare -- BASH="/bin/bash"
declare -x PWD="/home/bashuser"
```

When run with the `-f` option instead of `-p`, `declare` prints any functions defined for your shell. If you have just started with Bash, you may not have any functions defined just yet.

We will learn more about how to use the `declare` builtin in Chapter 6, *Loops and Conditionals*.

The test, [, and [[commands

The `test` builtin command is used to evaluate conditional expressions; it tests whether two strings are equal, whether a file exists, whether a string is empty, and other functions. The complete list of tests is available with `help test`.

For example, to test whether a file exists, you might use the following:

```
$ test -e /etc/passwd && echo 'Password file exists!'
Password file exists!
```

There is an alternative way to write this command, called `[`. No, that's not a typo; `[` is the name of the command! We can see this with `type`; there's even a program on our filesystem by the same name:

```
bash$ type -a [
[ is a shell builtin
[ is /usr/bin/[
```

The primary difference between `test` and `[` is that `[` requires its last argument to be `]`. The result is that it looks like a pair of square brackets surrounding the condition:

```
$ [ -e /etc/passwd ] && echo 'Password file exists!'
```

Because this syntax is confusing and can be hard to understand, Bash implements a new version of `[` called `[[`. It's actually not really a command; again, `type` can tell us the whole truth:

```
bash$ type [[
[[ is a shell keyword
```

In Bash scripts, you are not likely to need `test` very much, if ever, but you will definitely need the `[[` keyword that in turn derives its syntax from the `[` command. Understanding the `test` and `[` commands and the unique way conditionals work in shell clarifies one of the most confusing parts of shell script behavior. We'll look at that in more detail in `Chapter 7`, *Scripts, Functions, and Aliases*.

Essential system commands

This category of commands refer to executable files that are almost definitely installed on your system, and not implemented in Bash itself. All of these commands are specified by the POSIX standard, and so systems that aim to implement that standard should have them available.

The ls command

The `ls` program prints human-readable listings of directories. By default, with no arguments, this list is just the names of each file in the current directory, printed horizontally for readability:

```
$ ls
books   documents   music
```

If we add the `-a` flag, we can include *dot files* in our output, files beginning with a period:

```
$ ls -a
.   ..   .bashrc   .profile   books   documents   music
```

Note that this output includes the `.` and `..` entries, referring to the current and parent directory, respectively.

Using the `-l` option, which can be combined with `-a`, we can get a long listing of files:

```
$ ls -al
drwxr-xr-x 91 bashuser   bashuser   16384 Jul  7 19:50 .
drwxr-xr-x  5 root       root        4096 Jun  1 20:28 ..
-rw-r--r--  1 bashuser   bashuser    3391 Jun 30 01:03 .bashrc
-rw-r--r--  1 bashuser   bashuser     571 Jun 30 01:03 .profile
drwxr-xr-x 54 bashuser   bashuser    4096 Feb  6 14:54 books
drwxr-xr-x  2 bashuser   bashuser    4096 Nov 29  2014 documents
drwxr-xr-x 33 bashuser   bashuser    4096 Jun  4 00:06 music
```

Which columns are returned and the format the data takes varies depending on which options you provide, the system's configuration, your personal configuration, and which version of `ls` is installed.

Getting filename lists without ls

`ls` is a very useful command for getting listings, but it is often misused by being *parsed* in scripts to get filenames or file data from the output. The problem with this is that `ls` is designed for *human users* to read, not other programs.

You may have seen bad code like this on the web:

```
# Bad code
$ grep pattern `ls`
$ for file in `ls` ; do grep pattern $file ; done
```

This fails as soon as there is a filename with any special characters in it, such as a space, an asterisk, or a semicolon:

```
$ ls -1
programming
recipes
file with spaces
file*
# Bad code
$ grep pattern $(ls)
grep: file: No such file or directory
grep: with: No such file or directory
grep: spaces: No such file or directory
```

It is always better to use globs or `find` in this situation. If you only have to deal with one directory, use globs, as the commands tend to be simpler:

```
$ grep pattern -- *
$ find . -type f -exec grep pattern -- {} \;
```

You can loop over globs the same way with `for`:

```
$ for file in * ; do grep -F pattern -- "$file" ; done
```

We'll learn more about globs in `Chapter 5`, *Variables and Patterns*, and build on that for loops in `Chapter 6`, *Loops and Conditionals*.

To summarize: never use `ls` in scripts unless it's only for a human running your script to read. Resist the temptation to parse the output yourself, and look for a safer way to do it instead.

The mv command

The `mv` command moves files or directories to a new directory, or renames them in their existing one:

```
$ mv file path/to/directory
$ mv file1 file2
```

If the last argument is a directory, all of the arguments before it are moved into it, allowing you to move several files at once:

```
$ mv file1 file2 dir1 path/to/directory
```

Note that `mv` overwrites any existing file at its destination, by design. When you're using this interactively, if you don't expect to be overwriting files, the `-i` switch can be used to prompt you before you overwrite a file:

```
$ ls
customers-new   customers
$ mv -i customers-new customers
mv: overwrite 'customers'?
```

If you enter `y` at this prompt and press *Enter*, the overwrite will proceed. This feature is designed for user interaction, so in scripts, it may be better to test for the existence of the destination file before calling `mv`, and handling it an appropriate way:

```
#!/bin/bash
if [[ -e customers ]] ; then
    printf 'Customers file already exists, renaming\n'
    mv customers customers-old
fi
mv customers-new customers
```

The preceding script would move `customers` to `customers-old` first, if the target file already exists.

The cp command

The `cp` command is used to copy a file or set of files to a target directory, optionally providing it with a new name:

```
$ ls
oldfile
$ cp oldfile newfile
$ ls
oldfile    newfile
```

The new file in this case is truly a **copy**; you can change data in either the old or new file, and it won't affect data in the other.

 You can produce files that are **linked** rather than copied with the `ln` command; editing one name for the file will also change the content for all of its linked names.

If you specify more than two arguments after the options, with the last one being a directory, `cp` will copy *all* of the files before the last one into the directory name in the last argument:

```
$ cp file1 file2 file3 dir
```

`cp` with no options cannot copy directories or whole directory trees, and may give you an error message if it fails. The following output is from the GNU version of `cp`, referring to the non-standard `-r` option:

```
$ ls
olddir
$ cp olddir newdir
cp: -r not specified; omitting directory 'olddir'
```

If you provide the standardized `-R` option, you can copy a directory and all of the files beneath it:

```
$ cp -R olddir newdir
```

The GNU `cp`, which you are probably using if you're running GNU/Linux, includes a `-v` switch that shows each name as it's printed. This is particularly useful along with `-R`. Other versions of `cp`, such as those installed by default on BSD systems, may lack this option.

```
$ cp -Rv olddir newdir
'olddir' -> 'newdir'
'olddir/file1' -> 'newdir/file1'
```

```
'olddir/file2' -> 'newdir/file2'
'olddir/file3' -> 'newdir/file3'
```

The rm and rmdir commands

The rm tool deletes files, and directories if specified. Because it involves data loss by definition, shell script programmers should be very careful with this command:

```
$ ls
file1   file2   file3
$ rm file1 file2
$ ls
file3
```

Note that by default, rm does not remove directories:

```
$ mkdir mydir
$ rm mydir
rm: cannot remove 'mydir': Is a directory
```

You can force this with the standard -R or -r option, but it's safer to use rmdir. This is because rmdir will refuse to delete a directory if it still has files in it; it only deletes *empty* directories:

```
$ mkdir test1 test2
$ touch test1/file test2/file
$ rm -r test1
$ rmdir test2
rmdir: failed to remove 'test2': Directory not empty
```

We recommend you avoid the -R or -r flag where you can, and instead select files for deletion one by one. As a general rule of thumb in shell scripts, you should delete as *little* as possible, and as *specifically* as possible. If you carefully define what you're deleting and under what circumstances, you reduce the risk of unexpected problems. Emptying a directory manually of the files you expect to be there with rm first, and then attem

pting to clear it with rmdir, is a safe approach.

We'll learn more approaches to safely managing and d

eleting files in hierarchies in Chapter 8, *Best Practices*.

The grep command

The `grep` command matches **regular expression** patterns against lines of input data. Regular expressions are a compact string syntax that can be used to describe patterns in text. They can be simple text strings, such as `telnet`, which will match any lines that have those six exact letters in sequence:

```
$ grep 'telnet' /etc/services
telnet    23/tcp
rtelnet   107/tcp      # Remote Telnet
rtelnet   107/udp
telnets   992/tcp      # Telnet over SSL
tfido     60177/tcp  # fidonet EMSI over telnet
```

We could use some regular expression properties to filter this data more precisely. For example, to limit the output only to lines that *begin* with the word `telnet`, we could use the ^ metacharacter:

```
$ grep '^telnet' /etc/services
telnet    23/tcp
telnets   992/tcp      # Telnet over SSL
```

To limit the output to lines that *end* with `telnet`, we could use the $ metacharacter:

```
$ grep 'telnet$' /etc/services
tfido     60177/tcp  # fidonet EMSI over telnet
```

There are other metacharacters useful in even basic regular expressions. We'll look at more of them in detail in `Chapter 6`, *Loops and Conditionals*, including a way to match regular expressions in Bash itself, without using external tools.

Metacharacters in both `grep` and Bash itself can be confusing. We recommend you put your `grep` patterns in single quotes for clarity if they contain anything but numbers and letters, so that Bash will treat them as simple strings, and will pass them unchanged to `grep`.

By default, `grep` prints any lines in its input that match the pattern, in the same order in which it read them. It does not sort the output, or check it for uniqueness – you may need `sort` or `uniq` for that.

One of the common uses for `grep` in shell scripts is with the `-q` switch, which suppresses its output. This is useful for testing whether a file or input stream matches expressions without actually printing the matching lines, because `grep` exits with success (`0`) when it finds at least one pattern, and with failure (`1`) when it doesn't:

```
$ grep -q telnet /etc/services && echo 'Matched!'
Matched!
$ echo $?
0
$ grep -q foobar /etc/services && echo 'Matched!'
$ echo $?
1
```

There are a few other useful switches to `grep` specified by POSIX that are worth mentioning.

The `-c` switch prints a *count* of the matching lines, and not the lines themselves:

```
$ grep -c telnet /etc/services
5
```

The `-e` switch allows you to specify multiple patterns to match in the text. If we wanted to match `telnet` *or* `ssh` in the `services` file, we could write that like this:

```
$ grep -e ssh -e telnet /etc/services
```

Note that the lines do not have to match *both* expressions to be printed; they only have to match one.

The `-F` switch allows you to search for simple text strings with no special meaning. This is one way to allow you to search for a literal dollar sign, for example, without it meaning "end of line" as it otherwise would:

```
$ grep -F '$' monthly-costs
```

Note that we still have to put it in single quotes, to stop Bash's special meaning for `$` from interfering!

Finally, the `-v` switch can be used to *invert* the match, printing lines only if they *don't* match the pattern. For example, this prints the `/etc/services` file with no comment lines:

```
$ grep -v '^#' /etc/services
```

Most of the `grep` switches can be combined with one another. For example, to count all the lines in /etc/shells that don't have the bash or . fixed strings in them, we could write:

```
$ grep -cFv -e bash -e '.' /etc/shells
5
```

If you're using GNU/Linux, you are probably using GNU `grep`, which has many extended features; check out man grep to see them all.

The cut command

The `cut` command is most often used to select single columns of data from input separated by a single character, such as an /etc/passwd file. For example, this command line prints the home directories of every user on a GNU/Linux system:

```
$ cut -d: -f6 /etc/passwd
/root
/usr/sbin
/bin
. . .
```

In this example, −d specifies the **delimiter** or separator variable, in this case a colon, and −f specifies the number of the **field** (or column), starting from 1.

We can also specify the field numbers with hyphen-separated ranges, and/or comma-separated indices:

```
$ cut -d: -f1,6 /etc/passwd
root:/root
daemon:/usr/sbin
bin:/bin
. . .
$ cut -d: -f1,3-4 /etc/passwd
root:0:0
daemon:1:1
bin:2:2
. . .
```

We can leave one of the numbers out of a range, to mean "up to" or "from":

```
$ cut -d: -f-2 /etc/passwd
root:x
daemon:x
bin:x
. . .
```

```
$ cut -d: -f6- /etc/passwd
/root:/bin/bash
/usr/sbin:/usr/sbin/nologin
/bin:/usr/sbin/nologin
```

However, `cut` is not limited to delimited data. It can also split on character counts with `-c`, or bytes with `-b`. This can be a useful way to get only a certain number or range of bytes per line:

```
$ sha256sum .bashrc
50b9745d456e3023a859f3dd2e866e3a3a19a16b0af04b89e3387846fa158206  .bashrc
$ sha256sum .bashrc | cut -c-8
50b9745d
$ sha256sum .bashrc | cut -c9-16
456e3023a859f3dd
```

The wc command

The `wc` (word count) command counts lines, words, and bytes of its input. The default output is to show all three:

```
$ wc .bashrc
 101   550 3391 .bashrc
```

In this example, our `.bashrc` file has 101 lines, 550 space-delimited words, and 3,391 bytes. You can print only one of these numbers with the `-l`, `-w`, and `-c` options, respectively.

Technically, `wc -l` counts the number of newlines in the file, not the number of lines that they delimit. This is almost the same thing, but not exactly.

If you provide more than one file for `wc` to examine, it will also print a total:

```
$ wc -c .bashrc .bash_profile
3391 .bashrc
 471 .bash_profile
3862 total
```

Be careful to distinguish between *bytes* and *characters*. If you actually need to count the number of characters, for example if you're dealing with a file with Japanese characters or emojis in it, you can use the `-m` option instead:

```
$ wc -m -c japanese
 6 16 japanese
```

Note here that the number of characters (6) is different from the number of bytes (16), as some of the characters are composed of more than one byte in UTF-8 encoding.

 The character counts returned with the -m option will depend on your system's **locale** settings. Most modern systems will provide a UTF-8 locale to new users.

Getting file sizes with wc or du

wc with the -c option is a useful and portable way to get the size of a file (but not a directory) in bytes. The file does not have to be text for this to work:

```
$ wc -c /bin/bash
1099016
```

The output for the preceding command shows us that the /bin/bash binary is just over 1 MB in size.

The du program can show this information for a file or a directory, but its only portable unit size as specified in POSIX is 1 kibibyte (1024 bytes), with the -k option:

```
$ du -k /bin/bash
1076     /bin/bash
$ du -k /bin
13796    /bin
```

GNU du has a -b option, which does allow byte counts, but this is not **portable**, meaning you cannot rely on it working on all Unix-like systems.

The find command

The find command is a powerful way to operate recursively on a directory hierarchy. This means that you can provide it with a set of directories (or files), and it will apply appropriate tests and actions to them and also to any directories and files within them, such as children and grandchildren.

The default action for find is to print the filenames as it finds them:

```
$ find ~/recipes
/home/bashuser/recipes
/home/bashuser/recipes/lemon-garlic-fish.txt
/home/bashuser/recipes/japanese
```

```
/home/bashuser/recipes/japanese/katsu-curry.txt
/home/bashuser/recipes/gnocchi-and-sauce.doc
```

You can make this explicit with the -print action:

```
$ find ~/recipes -print
```

As long as there aren't too many files in the directory tree at that point, this can be a good way to get a complete file listing of your directory. Because find just prints the files as it finds them, you might want to run the output through sort if you want to read it:

```
$ find ~/recipes | sort
```

You can provide multiple directories to a find command; it will iterate through them all. You can also provide filenames directly on the command line. They will still be tested and have the actions run on them:

```
$ find ~/recipes ~/manuals todo.txt
```

You can filter the output for find in several ways. One of the most useful is using the -name option:

```
$ find ~/recipes -name '*fish*' -print
```

Using -name with this glob-style pattern will print the name of any file or directory that has the fish string in its filename. We could further refine this by adding the -type test, with the f flag to limit the recipes to files:

```
$ find ~/recipes -name '*fish*' -type f -print
```

Note that the directories or filenames to search always come first on the command line, and the filters always come before the actions.

To find files based on their modification date, you can use the -mtime test, with a minus (–) or plus (+) prefix for the following number. To find files modified more than three days ago, you could write:

```
$ find ~/recipes -mtime +3 -print
```

To find files modified less than five days ago:

```
$ find ~/recipes -mtime -5 -print
```

You can negate any of these filters with a single exclamation mark. For example, to find the names of files that do *not* match the string chicken:

```
$ find ~/recipes ! -name '*chicken*'
```

Be careful to make ! a word of its own, with at least one space on both sides, otherwise you might trigger unwanted history expansion.

If there is a subdirectory you wish to ignore somewhere in the tree, you can do this with the -prune action, which stops the descent at that point and continues with the rest of the tree. This can be a useful way of excluding metadata, such as Git or Subversion directories:

```
$ find myproject -name '.git*' -prune -o -print
```

In the preceding command line, -o print ("or print") prints the names of found files and directories that are *not* within a .git directory.

Executing commands for each result

Perhaps the most powerful action available in find is -exec, which allows you to run a command on each of the found results. This is best explained by an example; this command looks for occurrences of the search string in all files with names ending in .vim in a directory named vim:

```
$ find vim -type f -name '*.vim' -exec grep -F search -- {} \;
```

The -exec action here is followed by the name of the grep tool, its -F option, a "search" pattern, an option terminator (--), and two special arguments:

- {}: Replaced with each find result
- \;: Terminates the command

Note that we have to **escape** the semicolon with a backslash, in order to prevent Bash from interpreting it itself. Putting it in single quotes or double quotes would also work.

Suppose find found three matching files with the conditions we gave it:

```
$ find vim -type f -name '*.vim'
vim/config/main.vim
vim/maps.vim
vim/patterns.vim
```

Adding the -exec command line does the same thing as if our grep command were run over each of those files. It's like running these three commands:

```
$ grep -F search -- vim/config/main.vim
$ grep -F search -- vim/maps/vim
$ grep -F search -- vim/patterns/vim
```

If we change the command terminator to a plus sign (+), we can change the behavior to put as many of the arguments as possible on one line. This can be easier and more efficient for programs that can accept more than one filename argument:

```
$ find vim -type f -name '*.vim' -exec grep -F search -- {} +
```

The preceding command is like running this:

```
$ grep -F search -- vim/config/main.vim vim/maps/vim vim/patterns/vim
```

 Knowing how to use find well is one of the best "secret weapons" a GNU/Linux system administrator can have. We recommend you learn it thoroughly and practice so you understand how it works.

A note about find and xargs

You can find lots of advice online, and in some Bash books, about using a program called xargs to accomplish something similar to the -exec action of find:

```
$ find vim -type f -name '*.vim' | xargs grep -F search --
```

Using -exec for this sort of situation instead should be possible one way or another with some careful programming, and it's safer and more portable too, because the only safe way to use xargs is with the non-standard find -print0 and xargs -0 options that specify **null-byte terminators** between each file, to safely and correctly deal with filenames that contain newlines:

```
$ find vim -type f -name '*.vim' -print0 | xargs -0 grep -F search --
```

 Yes, file names on Unix can contain newlines, not just spaces. If your find command is going through a directory of files controlled by someone else, it's especially important to accommodate this, as it will break your script.

The sort and uniq commands

The `sort` command reads its input and writes it out again with the lines sorted, by default, alphanumerically by the first column. Like most filter commands that came with Unix, the input can come from a pipe, from files, or from data typed at the terminal. The first two forms are the most useful:

```
$ sort /etc/shells
$ sort ~/file1 ~/file2
$ printf '%s\n' 'Line 2' 'Line1' | sort
```

`sort` can sort data according to a particular column of its input data. For example, to sort all the entries in `/etc/passwd` by home directory (column 6), we could write:

```
$ sort -t: -k6,6 /etc/passwd
```

The options used here are:

- `-t`: Specifies the **delimiter** for the data that separates the columns, in this case a colon.
- `-k6,6`: Specifies by which column the data should be sorted, starting at one, in this case the sixth column. We add `,6` to specify that *only* the sixth column should be sorted; the remaining columns should not be used to sort.

Some useful options to modify each column:

- `-n`: Performs a numeric rather than alphabetical sort, so that "10" filters after "9," not before. Forgetting this is a common source of `sort` errors!
- `-r`: Reverses the sort order; shows the results that would be last first.

You can combine these formats to specify very precisely how you'd like to sort:

```
$ sort -t: -k7,7 -k3,3nr -k4,4nr /etc/passwd
```

This sorts the users file by login shell first, and for users with the same login shell, sorts them numerically, first by user ID, and then by group ID, in descending order.

You can also use the `-c` option simply to check whether the data is sorted. Some Unix filter tools, such as `uniq` and `comm`, require the data to be sorted to work correctly, and may print a warning if they find data arrives in an order they didn't expect. In practice, it's usually easier just to `sort` the data on the fly and then pass it into these tools.

Another useful option to note here is the −u option, which filters the data uniquely, ignoring any lines that have keys they've already seen. This surprises some shell script programmers who are accustomed to using uniq to do this; it's more flexible, because you can apply it to individual columns:

```
$ cat lyrics
02 the
03 air
02 later
02 often
01 in
04 tonight
04 for
00 something
$ sort −k1,1n −u lyrics
00 something
01 in
02 the
03 air
04 tonight
```

Despite the availability of the −u flag for sort, the uniq tool does still have some uses; perhaps the most useful one is with the −c flag, which allows us to count occurrences of each line of sorted data:

```
$ cat ips
192.2.0.1
192.2.0.1
192.2.0.25
192.2.0.1
192.2.0.24
192.2.0.1
192.2.0.25
$ sort ips | uniq −c
   4 192.2.0.1
   1 192.2.0.24
   2 192.2.0.25
```

The preceding output shows us that the IP address 192.2.0.1 occurred in the data four times, 192.2.0.25 twice, and 192.2.0.1 only once. If you looked at the output and thought, "we could sort by the first column," you're thinking like a shell programmer:

```
$ sort ips | uniq −c | sort −k1,1nr
   4 192.2.0.1
   2 192.2.0.25
   1 192.2.0.24
```

In this example, `-k1,1` is optional. Can you see why?

Summary

Because a typical shell script calls so many different commands, knowing the commands provided to you by the Bash shell itself, and by the system on which it runs, equips you to choose the right tool for the job; that decision can be particularly difficult in shell scripting, with so many options and alternatives available.

Knowing what the Bash shell provides – and what the POSIX standard *specifies* for the system to provide – will help you write shell scripts that will run safely, reliably, and portably on the systems where you need them to run. Tools like `type`, `help`, and `man` will enable you to identify and find the correct documentation for these commands.

In the next chapter, we'll look at how we can specify and redirect input and output for these and other commands, allowing you to pass just the data you need to them, just when you need it.

Input, Output, and Redirection

4

In this chapter, we'll look at how to manage **input** and **output** for Bash commands, specifying where any input *into* a command should come from, and where any output or errors *from* it should go. We can manage each of these using Bash's support for classic shell **redirection**, specifying a source or a destination for the data in the form of a path to a file.

In addition to file-based redirection, we'll also explore the use of **pipes** to transparently direct the output of one command straight into the input of another, a powerful means of **composing** (or combining) programs by having them work together. We'll also take a brief look at some general data-filtering possibilities using the sed and AWK programming languages.

In this chapter, we'll cover the following topics:

- Managing input and output from programs
- Controlling file-based redirection for both output and errors
- The basics of file-creation permissions
- Pipes between programs
- Advanced filtering possibilities with other programming languages

Redirecting output

When you enter a simple command that produces output in an interactive Bash session, such as a call to `printf`, it writes it straight back to your terminal so that you can read it, before returning you to your prompt:

```
$ printf 'Hello, terminal!\n'
Hello, terminal!
$
```

In both an interactive session and a script, you will often want to do something with the output besides printing it to the screen, particularly if you need to save the data permanently for later use. The simplest means of doing this is to save the output to a file.

To accomplish this, we can use one of Bash's **redirection operators**, the right angled bracket, >, followed by a filename path:

```
$ printf 'Hello, file!\n' > myfile
$
```

Notice that when we run the printf command in the preceding example, we don't get any output on the screen before our prompt shows again. However, if we run cat with myfile as its argument afterward, we can see where the command's output went; the file contains the output that the command would otherwise have written to our terminal:

```
$ cat myfile
Hello, file!
```

When you use output redirection to a file, the file is created even if the command had no output at all; if there's no output, it's created empty, or with a single terminating newline, depending on what the command emitted:

```
$ printf '' > myemptyfile
$ wc -c myemptyfile
0
```

Redirection paths

The path that comes after the redirection operator can include directory parts, and tildes to expand; both of the following redirections will work, if the mydir directory exists in your home directory:

```
$ cd
$ printf 'Hello, file!\n' > mydir/myfile
$ printf 'Hello, file!\n' > ~/mydir/myfile
```

Variables such as HOME can also be expanded for the file destination:

```
$ printf 'Hello, file!\n' > "$HOME"/myfile
```

For output redirection to a new file path to work, you will need permission to create files in the destination directory. If the file already exists, you will need permission to write to it in order to replace its contents. For example, if we try to write a file to the `root` user's home directory while we are not `root`, we will probably find this is not allowed:

```
$ printf 'Hello, root!\n' > ~root/myfile
bash: /root/myfile: Permission denied
```

Avoiding overwrites

You may have noticed in the output from the preceding commands that Bash does not prompt you about the destination file for an output redirection that doesn't exists – it creates it for you, without notifying you. Perhaps a bit more surprisingly, it won't prompt you if it *replaces* the contents of a file, either:

```
$ printf 'First command\n' > myfile
$ printf 'Second command\n' > myfile
$ cat myfile
Second command
```

The output from the first `printf` command is replaced with the output from the second `printf` command. If you don't want this to happen, and you only want to allow Bash to create *new* files, you can set the `-C` shell option with `set`:

```
$ set -C
```

For the running shell session, Bash will refuse to overwrite a file with a redirection operator:

```
$ printf 'Third command\n' > myfile
bash: myfile: cannot overwrite existing file
```

However, you can force it to write anyway with the `>|` syntax:

```
$ set -C
$ printf 'Third command\n' >| myfile
$
```

Don't forget that this only applies for your running shell. It doesn't prevent other running Bash shells or any other program from writing files. If you're writing a Bash script and you want to use the option, you need to include the `set -C` line near the top.

You may sometimes see the –C option referred to as `noclobber`. This is another Bash-specific name for the same option. We recommend –C, as it works in other shells, and is specified by POSIX.

Appending to files

If you wish to *add* output from a command to a file rather than replace it, double the right angled bracket to >>:

```
$ printf 'First command\n' > file
$ printf 'Second command\n' >> file
$ cat file
First command
Second command
```

The file doesn't need to exist already for this to work; the >> operator will create it for you, just like the > operator will.

This is a useful syntax for appending to log files, describing the output of your script as you go:

```
#!/bin/bash
printf 'Starting script\n' >> log
printf 'Creating test directory\n' >> log
mkdir test || exit
printf 'Changing into test directory\n' >> log
cd test || exit
printf 'Writing current date\n' >> log
date > date || exit
```

Understanding created file permissions

When Bash creates a new file on the system for you into which output has been directed, it needs to decide what **permissions** to set for the new file. It decides what those permissions should be with reference to a value called **umask** for the current process, which can be set by the process' owner.

The logic for how this decision is made is a little involved, and may require a quick review of how permissions on Unix-like systems work. To start, let's create a new file using an output redirection, and examine it with `ls -l`:

```
$ printf 'Hello, world\n' > myfile $ ls -l myfile -rw-r--r-- 1 bashuser
bashuser 1 2018-07-29 20:53:23 myfile
```

The permissions for the file are described in the the `-rw-r--r--` string at the start of each line. This is a human-readable version of the permissions; each character is either a letter flag or a dash. It's possible that your own value may differ, depending on your system's default settings:

- The first character of the string (–) is not a permission flag; it just shows the file type. In this case, a normal file (not a directory) shows a hyphen (–) in this field. A directory would show `d` instead.
- The next three characters (`rw-`) are the file **owner** permissions: **read**, **write**, and **execute**. Since you have just created the file, its owner will generally be you. In this example, the owner is able to read from and write to the file, but not to execute it as a program.
- The next three characters (`r--`) are the file **group** permissions: what a user in the file's group can do with the file if they're not the owner. In this case, members of our group can read the file, but can neither write to it nor execute it as a program.
- The last three characters (`r--`) are the permissions for the **world**, or any **other** users who are neither the file's owner, nor in its group. Again, these users can read our file, but cannot write to it or execute it.

If we have GNU `stat`, we can also examine the permissions in another, more compact, format; a numeric notation with three **octal** numbers ranging from 0 to 7:

```
$ stat -c %a myfile
644
```

This value is calculated by adding 4 for each *read* bit if set, 2 for each *write* bit if set, and 1 for each *execute* bit if set:

- The **owner** has read and write privileges, so the first value is `4 + 2`, or `6`
- The **group** has read privileges only, so the second value is just `4`
- The **world** has read privileges only, so the third value is just `4`

If we were to make the file executable by the owner, the owner permissions would add `1`, and would then be `7`, for numeric permissions of `744`.

This numeric format is not as easy for humans to read as the symbolic format, but it is closer to how the computer represents the permissions for files.

Choosing permissions for created files

While the defaults we saw in the previous section for newly-created files are sensible in many situations, they're not ideal in others. In particular, note that every other user on the system has permission to read the file, if they can get to it or name it. This isn't appropriate for files with sensitive information in them, such as passwords, private keys, or confidential user data. In such a situation, we *don't* want all the files we create to be readable by every user on the system, especially for the system users running processes for unauthenticated network services, such as a web server! How can we arrange for Bash to lock the files down?

When Bash creates files for redirected output, it starts with a permissions string of `rw-rw-rw-`, or in numeric notation, `666`: with those permissions, all the system's users could read or write the file. Before it creates the file, however, it checks the **umask** value of the process to find out which of those permissions it should *not* apply to the created file. This value therefore **masks** permissions bits. The `bash` program and many other system programs, such as `touch`, use umask to decide the default permissions for created files.

You can check the current umask value for your Bash shell with the `umask` command. By default, it prints in the numeric format. You can add the `-S` option to print the same value in string or **symbolic** form, if you find it easier to read:

```
$ umask
0022
$ umask -S
u=rwx,g=rx,o=rx
```

The value we see here, `0022`, is a common value for users who are not `root`. Note the extra zero at the start, a common prefix to signal an octal number. We can break down the other three digits like so:

- `0`: Don't strip any of the owner's privileges from the created file.
- `2`: Strip *write* permission for groups from the created file, but leave read and execute permissions intact.
- `2`: Strip *write* permission for all other users from the created file, but leave read and execute permissions intact.

We can change the umask value for the current running shell by providing it as an argument, in either numeric or symbolic format. To prevent users besides the file owner and group from being able to read the files, we might use a umask of 027:

```
$ umask 027
$ cat secrets > secret
$ ls -l secret
-rw-r----- 1 bashuser bashuser 1 2018-07-28 22:33:48 secret
```

In this case, other users – whose permissions are described by the last three flags in the permissions string – end up with no permissions for this file. If a user who is neither bashuser nor in the bashuser group tried to read the file, the kernel would refuse access, with Bash raising a "Permission denied" error.

By contrast, with an "empty" umask of 0000, Bash creates new files that are readable and writable for everyone:

```
$ umask 000
$ cat announcements > public
$ ls -l public
-rw-rw-rw- 1 bashuser bashuser 1 2018-07-28 22:36:08 public
```

If you're creating secret files during a shell session, consider switching to umask 077 to make new files readable only by you; similarly, when you are writing a new script, consider declaring an appropriate umask near the top.

Note that many other programs besides bash will also use umask for file creation, but not all of them do, and the umask doesn't prevent them from changing the permissions of the file after it's created. If you are using a new program for sensitive data, always check the permissions of any files it creates carefully.

Redirecting errors

If you experiment with redirecting the output of commands to files, you may find that error messages are still written to your terminal instead of the destination you specified:

```
$ grep pattern myfile /nonexistent > matches
grep: /nonexistent: No such file or directory
```

This is an intentional design feature of Unix-like operating systems, not just the `bash` program; it's to separate the output of commands (**standard output**, or `stdout`) from any error messages the command may also generate (**standard error**, or `stderr`). It's very common for commands to emit both output and error messages, so that the person running the script can read the errors without it interfering with any output from the script.

If you want to redirect error messages as well, the syntax is slightly different; you need to link the redirection operator with the standard error stream's **file descriptor** number, which is always `2`:

```
$ grep pattern myfile /nonexistent > matches 2> errors
$ cat errors
grep: /nonexistent: No such file or directory
```

Visually, we could present it like this:

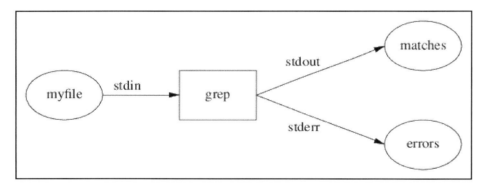

Note that just like redirecting standard output, the file will always be created, even if there is no error output. Also note that you can use `2>>` to *append* error output to a file; this is a useful way to keep a permanent error log for a script, because old errors in the file will not be overwritten the next time the script is run.

Combining errors with output

If you want to get both the output and errors from a command, you might try it this way at first:

```
$ grep pattern myfile /nonexistent > matches 2> matches
```

However, this does not do what you might expect; you might get only the output, or only the errors, or nothing at all, depending on the system. The syntax you want is to specify a file descriptor as the redirection target, using the ampersand (`&`), syntax to specify `1` (the standard output stream's descriptor):

```
$ grep pattern myfile /nonexistent > matches 2>&1
```

You can read the last word of this command line as "redirect standard error to the same place standard output is already going."

Note that the order matters here; you can't put `2>&1` before `> matches` to accomplish the same thing. Redirections are made in order, from left to right.

 There is another Bash-specific syntax, `&>`, to do the same thing, but the longer and more explicit method is the clearest to anyone reading your script, and works on shells besides Bash.

Blocking errors completely

A common idiom to ignore error output from commands is to discard it by directing it to the special `/dev/null` device file, which just ignores anything written to it and is always empty:

```
$ grep pattern myfile /nonexistent > matches 2> /dev/null
```

If you want to ignore error output, this works, but think carefully before you do this. Error messages are written to let you know and to help you understand when something is not working, and they assist in debugging, especially when the error isn't fatal – that is, when the command still runs to completion and maybe generates some output, so if nobody sees the errors, it might seem like everything is working fine.

A good example is the `comm` tool, which shows lines that differ between files, similar to `diff`, except it requires its input files to be *sorted* to do its efficient comparison. If they're not sorted the way it expects, it raises an error like this:

```
$ comm myfile1 myfile2
comm: file 1 is not in sorted order
```

This warning is to alert the user that the program actually cannot do its work correctly if the files are not sorted. If you suppress the error completely, and don't log it anywhere, it makes it much harder to debug later:

```
$ comm myfile1 myfile2 2> /dev/null
$ echo $?
1
```

We can see the `comm` command exited non-zero, meaning there was an error. What was the error? We can't tell, because we blocked it! This is particularly painful in automated scripts: nobody ever sees the error, so it could be a long time before anyone actually notices things are broken.

Instead, you may be able to adjust your script so that the error condition does not arise at all, or perhaps pass program-specific options (often `-f` or `-q`) to suppress errors selectively, instead of just discarding any and all error output.

Another method is to write the error output to a file, in case you do need to check it later:

```
$ grep pattern myfile /nonexistent > matches 2>> errorlog
```

Sending output to more than one place

If you need the output of a command in more than one place, and the command does not need to run for long, the most straightforward way is to save it to a single file first, and then use `cat` or `cp` to send it wherever it needs to be copied. This is simple and easy to read and understand, and is the recommended way to do it if the command does not need to run for long.

However, for situations where you want the output to go to more than one place while the command is actually running, you can use the `tee` command, which copies all of its input to any files named in its arguments:

```
$ printf 'Copy this output\n' | tee myfile
Copy this output
$ cat myfile
Copy this output
```

Notice that the output went to both the terminal and to `myfile`. This works when multiple files are specified, too:

```
$ printf 'Copy this output\n' | tee myfile1 myfile2 myfile3
Copy this output
$ ls myfile*
myfile1   myfile2   myfile3
```

Each of the three files will end up with the same content.

You can use the `-a` option of `tee` to *append* to files rather than overwriting them, much like using >> instead of >.

Redirecting input

Many commands invoked from Bash read their input from one or more files provided on the command line, particularly the classic Unix text filtering tools, such as `grep` and `sort`. When these commands are passed one or more filenames as arguments, they switch to reading their input from those files in the order they were specified, instead of from their own standard input:

```
$ grep pattern myfile1 myfile2 myfile3
$ sort -k1,1 myfile1 myfile2 myfile3
```

This tends to mean that you do not need to use Bash to redirect *input* as often as you need to redirect *output*, because well-designed Unix programs can usually change their input behavior by specifying filenames, without any shell syntax involved.

However, not all programs behave this way, and it will sometimes be necessary to use **input redirection** to specify the source for a command's input. For example, the `tr` Unix command is a simple way to translate characters in input to other characters, specified in sets. We can try it out on the command line to convert all lowercase ASCII letters to uppercase in each line we type:

```
$ tr a-z A-Z
Hello, world!
HELLO, WORLD!
```

If you are using a non-English locale, you might need to type `export LC_COLLATE=C` first for this to work.

If we wanted to do this with data from a file named `mylines`, we might try to write it like this:

```
$ tr a-z A-Z mylines
```

But that doesn't seem to work:

```
tr: extra operand 'mylines'
Try 'tr --help' for more information.
```

This is because the `tr` program doesn't check its arguments for files; it *only* reads the standard input stream, which by default comes from your terminal, so we need another way to specify input for the command.

Many shell programmers try to solve this problem with a `cat` pipe first, like this:

```
$ cat mylines | tr a-z A-Z
```

This works, but it's what we refer to as a **useless use of** `cat`; because we only have one file, there's nothing to combine, and hence no need to make `cat` read it for us. Instead, we can use the **input redirection operator**, <, directly with the `tr` command:

```
$ tr a-z A-Z < mylines
```

In this case, the shell will open the `mylines` file and use it as the source for standard input for the `tr` command.

Like the output redirection operator, >, we can place the input redirection operator, <, elsewhere on the command line, including at the very start; this works, but it's not very commonly used:

```
$ < mylines tr a-z A-Z
```

Note also that input redirection, output redirection, and error redirection can all be performed simultaneously for the same command line:

```
$ tr a-z A-Z < mylines > mylines.capitalized 2> mylines.error
```

The preceding command runs capitalization on input read from `mylines`, writing the output to the `mylines.capitalized` file and any errors to `mylines.error`.

Using a long string as input with here-documents

In some cases, you may have a long multi-line string for input to a command in your script that you don't want to separate into another file. This is often the case with output for -h or --help options, where you don't want to store the help information outside the script.

Because quoted strings can include multiple lines, we can just use printf for this; it works fine, emitting multiple lines of output:

```
#!/bin/bash
case $1 in
    -h|--help)
        printf '%s\n' 'foo command help:
-h, --help: Show this help
-q, --quiet: Run without diagnostics
-v, --verbose: Add extra diagnostics'
        exit 0
        ;;
esac
```

For commands that accept the data as input, such as cat, rather than in argument, such as printf, a different syntax can be used: a **here-document**, a kind of quoting that uses a token word or **delimiter** to specify where a document for a command's standard input should finish.

The preceding snippet could be rewritten to use a here-document in cat, instead of an argument to printf:

```
#!/bin/bash
case $1 in
    -h|--help)
        cat <<'EOF'
foo command help:
-h, --help: Show this help
-q, --quiet: Run without diagnostics
-v, --verbose: Add extra diagnostics
EOF
        exit 0
        ;;
esac
```

This includes as input to cat all lines that are *between* the <<'EOF' line and the next occurrence of the EOF token as the first word of a new line; in this case, this is a total of four lines of data, each terminated with a newline character. That data becomes the standard input to cat, which in turn prints it to the program's standard output.

Note the following details of this syntax:

- The redirection operator is two left angled brackets, <<. Having only one left angled bracket will trigger plain old file-input redirection – not what you intended!
- The lines in the data are not indented at the same level as the rest of the case structure. This is because the leading whitespace will be interpreted *literally*, and printed exactly as you write it. We say that leading whitespace is not *stripped*.
- Similarly, the **terminating** delimiter that flags the end of the here-document is the only content on the line, with no leading whitespace. If you include whitespace before the delimiter, the line is taken as part of the input.
- The token word, the **delimiter**, is EOF. This is only a common convention; it can be any string (if quoted).
- The delimiter is in **single quotes**. Similar to the behavior of single quotes, this specifies that until the EOF is reached, all of the characters in the data should be treated literally, including $.

If you want to expand variables or do command substitution inside a here-document, you can leave out the single quotes around the delimiter. The here-document then expands variables and substitutions inside it, much like a double-quoted string. This allows you to use values from the environment or elsewhere in the program in the string:

```
#!/bin/bash
cat <<EOF
Hello, $USER; you are running this program on $(hostname -s).
Your home directory is $HOME.
EOF
```

If you really want to indent your here-documents, there is an exception to the preceding rule about leading whitespace; if you include a hyphen between << and the delimiter, the tabs (but not spaces) at the front of your input lines will be ignored:

```
#!/bin/bash
cat <<-'EOF'
    Leading tabs
        will not be included in the output
EOF
```

Using pipes

In some cases, we may store *output* from one command in a file, with the intent to use it in the *input* to another. Consider this script, which accepts a list of ASCII words on its standard input, converts any uppercase letters to lowercase with tr, sorts them, and then prints a count of how often each word is used, sorted by frequency:

```
#!/bin/bash

# Convert all capital letters in the input to lowercase
tr A-Z a-z > words.lowercase

# Sort all the lowercase words in order
sort words.lowercase > words.sorted

# Print counts of how many times each word occurs
uniq -c words.sorted > words.frequency

# Sort that list by frequency, descending
sort -k1,1nr words.frequency
```

This sort of script involving many commands in sequence to filter and aggregate data can be very useful for analyzing large amounts of raw text, such as log files. However, there's a problem; when we run this, it leaves some files lying around:

```
$ ls words.*
words.frequency  words.lowercase  words.sorted
```

Of course, we could clean them up with rm at the end of the script:

```
rm words.frequency words.lowercase words.sorted
```

It would be preferable not to involve these temporary files in the first place, and instead to feed the output of each program directly into the input of the next one. This is done with the **pipe** operator. We can reduce the whole script to just one **pipeline**:

```
tr A-Z a-z | sort | uniq -c | sort -k1,1nr
```

Visually, we could represent it like this:

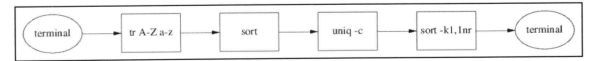

This pipeline accomplishes the same thing as the script does; try running it and type a few words separated by newlines, and then type `Control-D` to terminate it (**end-of-file**):

```
$ tr A-Z a-z | sort | uniq -c | sort -k1,1nr
bash
bash
script
user
script
Bash
SCRIPT
```

If *Ctrl + D* is pressed to finish the list, we get this output:

```
3 bash
3 script
1 user
```

You can think of the pipe operator as a way to perform input redirection (<) and output redirection (>) for a pair of programs *into one another*, like connecting things with a physical pipe, without having to involve an intermediate state, such as a file.

 Note that only the output from each command is redirected into the input of the next; pipes do not affect where errors are sent.

A convenient property of the pipe operator is that it can be used at the end of a line; we could put the preceding **pipeline** into a script spanning multiple lines, as follows:

```
#!/bin/bash
tr A-Z a-z |
sort |
uniq -c |
sort -k1,1nr
```

You may find this more readable, particularly if some of your commands are long.

Adding file contents to a stream

Sometimes, you may want to add header or footer information to a stream in a pipeline, perhaps read from another file. One straightforward way of doing this is using `cat` for its intended purpose of concatenating streams of input.

Normally, cat combines all of the filenames specified in its arguments and writes them to standard output, in the same order they were specified:

```
$ cat myfile1 myfile2 myfile3 > myfiles.combined
```

We can use the special value of a single hyphen (–) anywhere among the cat filename arguments to denote that any *standard input* to cat should be added at that point. For example, if we had a generate-html command that generated the body of an HTML document, we might want to add the headers with the <!DOCTYPE html>, <html>, <head>, <body>, and other tags in header.html at the top, and the closing tags, such as </body> and </html>, in footer.html at the end. We could combine them with one pipeline using the – representation for the standard input:

```
$ generate-html
<p>Here is the content!</p>
$ generate-html | cat header.html - footer.html
<!DOCTYPE html>
<html>
    <head>
        <title></title>
    </head>
    <body>
<p>Here is the content!</p>
    </body>
</html>
```

Note that the single hyphen word (–) syntax is not a special value to Bash itself; it's just a conventional way for individual programs to specify the standard input stream on the command line. It's supported for many of the standardized POSIX tools, such as cat. For some other commands, you might need to explicitly use the pseudo-device file, /dev/stdin, in place of the hyphen.

Piping output from multiple programs

With what we've learned so far, it's easy to combine the output of two separate commands into a file; we just run them in the appropriate sequence, and use the redirection output with >> to append the data:

```
$ date > myout
$ hostname >> myout
$ cat myout
Mon Jul 30 21:32:33 NZST 2018
bashserver.example.net.
```

However, it may not be clear how you could combine two *streams* of output from commands into one without saving them into a temporary file, for example to capitalize all of the letters within it with `tr`. There isn't a specific syntax to "merge" pipes.

There is still a way to do this without resorting to a temporary file; you can use a **compound command** that contains all of the commands for output redirection, and apply the redirection to that compound command, rather than to the individual commands within it.

The most straightforward way to do this is with a **group command**, which is delimited with curly brackets, { and }:

```
$ { date ; hostname ; } | tr a-z A-Z
MON JUL 30 21:38:52 NZST 2018
BASHSERVER.EXAMPLE.NET.
```

Note that we not only had to separate the `date` and `hostname` commands here with a semicolon, we also had to include a semicolon control operator for the final command to terminate it, before closing the group with }. This form of compound command is the same as the one commonly used for functions, as we'll see in Chapter 7, *Scripts, Functions, and Aliases*.

Input and output redirection can also apply to compound commands:

```
$ { date ; printf '%s\n' apple carrot banana ; } > mywords
$ { read date ; printf '%s\n' "$date" ; sort ; } < mywords
```

There are other kinds of compound commands, which we'll learn about in Chapter 6, *Loops and Conditionals*, for which redirection works just as well. This property of redirection for compound commands is the basis of Bash's `while read -r` loop idiom, for reading a file line-by-line.

Filtering programs

When we establish long pipelines, we sometimes want to add an extra "link" into the pipeline to reformat or filter the data in some way before passing it on to the next program, and we may find that there are no programs available to us on the system that filter the text in exactly the way we need.

We may therefore wish to use something with a bit more power; we'll look at the sed and AWK programming language interpreters, both of which are specified by POSIX. They are ideal tools to write short one-line programs dedicated to filtering text streams in novel ways.

We can't completely explain sed and AWK here, but we'll give some examples that will demonstrate the sort of tasks for which they are ideal. Like many other commands useful in Bash scripts, neither of these programs are part of Bash itself; they're just very often used in Bash and other shell script command lines.

The sed stream editor

The sed program is an interpreter for sed, the **stream editor**, a simple data-driven programming language that accepts data on input (normally strings), and acts on and transforms it conditionally. The programs end up being very short, as the commands are all only one letter long. This terse approach means they fit very well on a command line and are quick to type.

We'll use the following example file, named manual, for our sed demonstration:

```
$ cat manual
The sed utility is a stream editor that shall read one or more text files,
make editing changes according to a script of editing commands,
and write the results to standard output.
```

With an empty program, sed simply reproduces all of the output without changing it; this is because by default it prints all the lines it filters implicitly, unless they are deleted:

```
$ sed '' manual
The sed utility is a stream editor that shall read one or more text files,
make editing changes according to a script of editing commands,
and write the results to standard output.
```

Note the empty string is specified with ' '; if we don't use the quotes to show an empty argument, sed will only be passed manual as an argument, and will think it's a script!

We can delete individual lines with the d command, by prefixing them with the line number:

```
$ sed '1d' manual
make editing changes according to a script of editing commands,
and write the results to standard output.
```

We can delete a *range* of lines with a comma-separated pair of numbers:

```
$ sed '1,2d' manual
and write the results to standard output.
```

Lines can be selected not just with line numbers, but also with pattern matches. For example, to delete all lines from "1" up to and including the next occurrence of the word "commands," we could write the following:

```
$ sed '1,/commands/d' manual
and write the results to standard output.
```

We can transform lines with the `s` command, which substitutes a regular expression pattern into a given replacement:

```
$ sed 's/stream/river/' manual
The sed utility is a river editor that shall read one or more text files,
...
```

The `s/pattern/replacement/` pattern-replacement syntax is the function of sed that is best known to programmers even outside of shell scripting; it shows up very often in older shell scripts, and in various other contexts in Unix, such as in the `vi` editor.

These are just a few examples of the text transformations possible with sed; you should check your operating system's manual page for more details.

While powerful, the terseness of these examples shows sed programs can be a little hard to write at first. Fortunately, many of the most common filtering functions for which programmers often use sed can be done in Bash itself, using **parameter expansion** for common string operations such as removing extensions or leading paths from paths. We will discuss that in `Chapter 5`, *Variables and Patterns* .

Don't be tempted to use sed for tasks such as parsing programming languages or markup languages such as HTML; it's just not powerful enough to do it correctly! Use a proper parser such as HTML's `tidy` instead, and keep sed programs for simple and well-defined line-based text translations. For XML, try `xpath`; for JSON, try `jq`.

The AWK programming language

The AWK programming language interpreter works in many ways like `sed`; it accepts (by default) lines of input, performs pattern-matching and filtering on each, and applies actions based on those patterns.

AWK is especially well-suited for data that takes the form of a regular pattern of words, or **fields**, which makes it ideal for filtering data in clearly-delineated columns. By default, fields are separated by any whitespace (spaces or tabs), and records are separated by newlines, but both of these can be changed as part of the program.

The basic form of an AWK program is a set of **patterns** for each record (normally a line) to match, for which an **action** is performed for each matching record. We will take a look at some simple examples so you can get an idea of the kinds of patterns and actions that are possible.

We'll use the following `groceries` data file for our example AWK programs:

```
$ cat groceries
Item     Quantity  Price
Apples   5         0.50
Cereal   1         3.40
Soda     2         1.10
```

The best-known application of AWK for administrators and programmers is to extract a single column of data. We can do this with a `print` command and by specifying the second column with `$2`:

```
$ awk '{ print $2 }' groceries
Quantity
5
1
2
```

We can also print *multiple* columns by separating them with commas:

```
$ awk '{ print $2, $3 }' groceries
Quantity  Price
5         0.50
1         3.40
2         1.10
```

If we want to exclude the first line with the headers so that we only retrieve the number data, we can do that as part of the AWK program too, by specifying a condition as the pattern preceding the action:

```
$ awk 'NR > 1 { print $2, $3 }' groceries
5         0.50
1         3.40
2         1.10
```

`NR` in the preceding command refers to the record number, in this case the same as the line number, and specifies that the second and third columns should only be printed if the record number is greater than `1`, thereby skipping the headers.

We can even do some arithmetic, calculating the total price for each item by multiplying the unit price by the quantity, then formatting them and prefixing them with a dollar sign using printf:

```
$ awk 'NR > 1 { printf "$%.2f\n", $2 * $3 }' groceries
$2.50
$3.40
$2.20
```

 Note that printf in the Awk program is implemented by AWK; it's not the Bash command of the same name!

As with sed, these examples only scratch the surface; AWK is a small programming language, but it has many features beyond merely filtering by column number. Consult the documentation for your system's version of awk to get a better idea of what it can do. Note that different versions of AWK support different extensions to the POSIX standard; keep your AWK programs simple, if you can!

Summary

While the model of standard input, output, and error streams for Bash is simple in principle, redirections and piping allow us to combine programs and files in novel ways to efficiently and expressively program in only one or two lines what might take hundreds of lines in other programming languages. This is especially true when extended to applying other programming languages, such as sed or AWK, to filter data appropriately.

In the next chapter, we'll learn how to gather and manipulate data *within* Bash itself, using its builtin variables and patterns.

5

Variables and Patterns

In this chapter, we'll learn how to work with data and variables in Bash, and how to use them with pattern matching and shell glob syntax. While you can get a lot done by just piping existing commands together, we often need variables to get more fine-tuned behavior from scripts.

We'll cover:

- Variable declarations and scope
- Environment variables
- String operations
- Arithmetic expressions
- Capturing program output in a variable
- Matching filenames with glob patterns
- Using arrays and associative arrays

Using variables

The basic form of a variable assignment in shell script looks like this:

```
myshell='GNU Bourne-Again shell'
```

This declares a variable named `myshell`, and gives it the string contents *GNU Bourne-Again shell*.

Note that there is no space either before or after the equals sign, as there might be in a C-like language. Note also that the value in this example assignment is surrounded by **single quotes**, so the contents are interpreted literally, without expanding any special characters, in this case spaces. As with other single-quoted strings in shell script, the quotes themselves do not become part of the value.

You will need to quote any value that contains special characters in variable assignments. For new shell programmers, it is safest to quote *all* the values in their assignments; it might be unnecessary in some cases, but it doesn't do any harm, and it's easier to manage:

```
myshell='sh'
myvar='GNU'\''s Not Unix!'
myprompt="$USER@$HOST"
```

By design, you can't assign parameters such as $1, $?, or $#; they are read-only variables that are managed by the shell. Trying to assign to them will yield strange errors, or even no output at all.

See the "Special Parameters" section of the Bash manual page to learn more about these special parameters. We'll be using a few of them in later chapters.

Listing variables

After a variable has been assigned a value, you can check it by using `printf` or `echo`:

```
$ today='August 9th'
$ printf '%s\n' "$today"
August 9th
```

Bash includes a builtin named `declare`, which can be used with variable names as its argument to show more information about each named variable and its value:

```
$ declare -p today
declare -- today='August 9th'
```

In this case, the `--` string in the output tells us that there is no special attribute to this variable.

You can list all of the variables currently assigned by leaving out the name:

```
$ declare -p
declare -- BASH="/bin/bash"
declare -r BASHOPTS="cdspell:checkhash..."
declare -ir BASHPID
declare -- PS1="\\u@\\h:\\w\\$ "
...
```

Naming variables

A variable name in bash must begin with a letter or an underscore, and can be followed by any letter or number, or more underscores.

These variables names are all legal:

- `myvar`
- `MYVAR`
- `Myvar`
- `mYVAR`
- `_myvar`
- `my_var`
- `myvar_`
- `my012`

These variable names are not allowed:

- `1myvar`
- `my-var`
- `my.var`
- `my:var`

Variable name case

Note that in our example assignments earlier, variable names such as `myshell` and `today` are in *lowercase*. Very often, when you read shell scripts others have written, particularly older scripts, you will find that variables that are used only internally in the script are written in *uppercase*, such as `MYSHELL`.

The issue with using the `ALL_UPPERCASE` variable names for your own script variables is that environment variables, such as `HOME`, and shell internal variables, such as `BASH_VERSION`, are also (almost) always written in uppercase, and there are a lot of them – so if you use capitalized names, there is a significant risk of accidentally breaking an important variable in your own script.

For example, if you were to assign PATH rather than path for one of your variables, you would change the environment variable that the system uses to find other programs:

```
#!/bin/sh
PATH=/home/bashuser/myfile
grep -- mystring "$PATH"
```

If this script is run, it yields:

grep: command not found

This is because with PATH changed to a filename, the system can no longer find the fundamental grep tool – and the error message doesn't make it clear why. Similar problems occur with names such as BASH_VERSION, SHELL, or even innocent-looking words such as RANDOM.

You can avoid this class of problems by naming variables for your script in all lowercase, since very few shell-internal and environment variables are written like this:

```
#!/bin/sh
path=/home/bashuser/myfille
grep -- mystring "$path"
```

There is one exception: the http_proxy environment variable used by some programs is always written lowercase, for historical reasons.

Of course, if you really do want to change one of these variables, you can still do so:

```
PATH="$PATH:/home/myuser/scripts"
MYDIR=/home/myuser
export MYDIR
```

Clearing variables

If you want to assign a variable an empty value, you can do so by leaving the right side of an assignment to the variable blank:

$ system=

However, the variable name still appears in the list of variables, it just has an empty value:

bash$ declare -p system
declare -- system=""

The `system` variable is *defined*, but *empty*. POSIX shell script actually does not make much of a distinction between these two states. It's more common to test whether a variable is empty than it is to check whether it's defined:

```bash
#!/bin/bash
# If the 'system' variable is not empty, print its value to the user
if [[ -n $system ]] ; then
    printf 'The "system" variable is: %s\n' "$system"
fi
```

You can actually *remove* a variable with `unset`:

```
$ unset -v system
$ declare -p system
bash: declare: system: not found
```

If you do ever need to check whether a variable is defined, Bash allows you to do this with the `-v` test; note that we use `system`, not `$system`, here:

```bash
#!/bin/bash
# If the "system" variable has been set--even if it's empty--print its
# value to the user
if [[ -v system ]] ; then
    printf 'The "system" variable is: %s\n' "$system"
fi
```

Environment variables

Variable assignments such as the ones we've done so far in this chapter are only visible to the current running shell. Their values don't implicitly affect a program called by the script – a **forked process**.

The easiest way to demonstrate this on the command line is to start another shell process after making an assignment. Consider this basic shell session, including an assignment to a variable named `realname`:

```
bash$ declare -p BASHPID
declare -ir BASHPID="7013"
bash$ realname='Bash User'
bash$ declare -p realname
declare -- realname='Bash User'
```

If we start a new bash process, we get a new process ID in BASHPID, and the realname variable does not show as a set:

```
bash$ bash
bash$ declare -p BASHPID
declare -ir BASHPID="7585"
bash$ declare -p realname
bash: declare: realname: not found
```

Once we use exit to return to the parent process, it shows as available again:

```
bash$ exit
bash$ declare -p BASHPID
declare -ir BASHPID="7013"
bash$ declare -p realname
declare -- realname='Bash User'
```

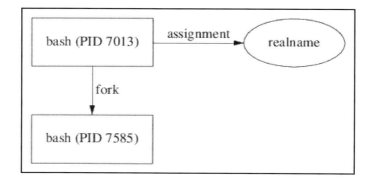

If you want a way for variables to be visible and usable by any of the programs you call on the script or command line, you need to use **environment variables**. The POSIX-specified command to do this is called export, which is a builtin command in Bash:

```
bash$ REALNAME='Bash User'
bash$ export REALNAME
bash$ declare -p REALNAME
declare -x REALNAME="Bash User"
```

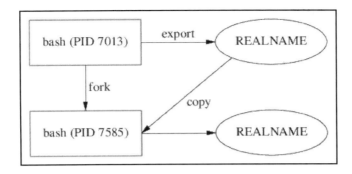

 We use the all-uppercase REALNAME here rather than realname, observing a convention for all-uppercase names for environment variables.

Notice that the declare output for the preceding command is slightly different from our system example; it includes the -x option, specifying that the REALNAME variable has been exported to the environment. This export makes the variable available to child processes:

```
bash$ bash
bash$ declare -p REALNAME
declare -x REALNAME="Bash User"
bash$ exit
```

You can get a list of all environment variables and their values with declare -x in Bash. The POSIX-specified env program is another option, called with no arguments, but you might want to sort its output in order to read it.

You should only export variables when you actually need to use their values in subprocesses. It may be tempting to export all of your variables, but it's untidy, and you risk overwriting an important environment variable used by a program without intending to, which can be hard to debug.

 Environment variables are simple string key-value pairs. You cannot reliably export a data structure like an array with environment variables.

Calling programs with environment variables

Environment variables are properties of *all* processes, not just `bash` processes. They can be read by other programming languages, such as C, Perl, Awk, or Python. This means that environment variables are sometimes used to affect how another program runs.

For example, the `sort` program uses **locale settings** to decide the sort order for some strings – specifically, it uses the `LANG` or `LC_COLLATE` environment variables. If `LC_COLLATE` is set to `en_US.UTF-8`, it will sort lowercase `a` before uppercase `A`:

```
$ printf '%s\n' 'alligator' 'Alfred' >words
$ LC_COLLATE=en_US.UTF-8
$ export LC_COLLATE
$ sort words
alligator
Alfred
```

However, if the environment variable is then set to `C`, its behavior changes:

```
$ LC_COLLATE=C
$ sort words
Alfred
alligator
```

There's a shortcut here: we can call a program with a modified environment by putting environment variable assignments *before* the call to the program, on the same line:

```
$ LC_COLLATE=C sort words
Alfred
alligator
```

This sets the `LC_COLLATE` environment variable to `C` for the `sort` call, but *doesn't* change it in the rest of the script.

This combination of assignment syntax and command-line call is very useful, but it's also not very intuitive, because the presence of a command after the variable assignments changes what the assignments mean more or less entirely. Make sure you understand the difference between these two lines:

```
mycollate=C
LC_COLLATE=C sort words
```

The first is defining a *shell* variable named `mycollate` to the value `C`. The second is defining only an *environment* variable, and only for the `sort` call that it starts on the `words` file, not the rest of the script.

Expanding variables

Bash, and shell scripting languages in general, refer to the process of evaluating variables and other parameters such as $1 as **parameter expansion**.

The safest way to use parameter expansion is to prefix the name of the variable with a dollar sign as part of a double-quoted string:

```
$ realname='Bash User'
$ printf '%s\n' "Hello, $realname."
Hello, Bash User.
```

If you need to distinguish the variable name from characters around it, you can use curly brackets:

```
$ printf '%s\n' "__Hello, ${realname}__"
__Hello, Bash User__
```

This prevents Bash from trying to expand a variable named `realname__`, with two trailing underscores.

Note that if you expand a variable that doesn't exist, by default Bash does not issue any warnings; it just replaces the variable with an empty string:

```
$ printf '%s\n' "Hello, $notset."
Hello, .
```

If you want to arrange for Bash to throw an error whenever an unset variable is expanded, you can use the -u option with set:

```
bash$ set -u
bash$ printf '%s\n' "Hello, $notset."
bash: notset: unbound variable
```

Reading a value into a variable

The `read` builtin command with its -r option can be used to read values into variables from standard input, including directly from the terminal:

```
$ read -r myname
Bash User
```

Press *Ctrl + D* (end-of-file) after pressing *Enter* after the last preceding line; the entire first line of input will be used as the value for `myname`:

```
bash$ declare -p myname
declare -- myname='Bash User'
```

You should always use the `-r` option with `read`, to avoid running into confusing issues with reading backslashed values.

We will use the `read` builtin a lot more in Chapter 6, *Loops and Conditionals*, as part of Bash's looping syntax for processing data.

Getting command output in variables

We can get command output in variables using **command substitution**. For example, to assign the output of the `whoami` command to the `myusername` variable, we could use the following:

```
$ myuser="$(whoami)"
$ printf '%s\n' "$myuser"
bashuser
```

Don't forget to use double quotes around the expansion, so that special characters, such as spaces and asterisks, don't get treated specially by the shell.

Command substitution has the special property of trimming *trailing newlines* from the output of the command it executes. The `whoami` command actually prints the current username, followed by a newline. Command substitution removes that trailing newline. This is simply for convenience, as the trailing newline is usually not wanted.

Command substitutions can be nested, but note that the double quotes are still required even on the inner expansion to suppress unwanted expansion:

```
$ mypwent="$(getent passwd "$(whoami)")"
```

Especially in older shell scripts, you may sometimes see backticks (` ) used for command substitution. Bash still allows this syntax so that older scripts can run, but you should prefer the `$(command)` syntax to `` `command` ``; the former is easier to read, and much easier to perform expansions within expansions.

Parameter expansion forms

Besides the simple "`$myvar`" form of parameter expansion, there are some other forms available for common string operations that can be very useful. Some of these forms are specified by the POSIX shell scripting standard, and others are specific to Bash itself; we will distinguish them with the `bash$` prompt for Bash-specific forms, and the single `$` prompt for POSIX-specified forms.

Specifying default values

If a variable may not have a value in a script, you can specify a default or "fallback" value for it with the form "`${myvar:-default}`", where `default` is the string you want to use instead of the variable's value if it's unset or blank. This can be useful for default directories that can be overridden by environment variables, if present:

```
cd -- "${MYSCRIPT_DIR:-/usr/local/myscript}"
...
```

This script will change into the directory named in the `MYSCRIPT_DIR` environment variable if set, or the `/usr/local/myscript` directory it it is not set, or if it is blank.

If you use the `:=` characters instead of `:-`, you can additionally assign the default value to the environment variable for the rest of the script:

```
cd -- "${MYSCRIPT_DIR:=/usr/local/myscript}"
...
```

If it was initially unset or blank, then after the first line of the preceding script, `MYSCRIPT_DIR` will additionally be set to `/usr/local/myscript` for the remainder of the script.

String chopping

There are also some ways to perform string "chopping" via parameter expansion, which are frequently useful for trimming paths. The "`${myvar#prefix}`" form removes one occurrence of `prefix` from the variable's expansion:

```
$ ta='type:json'
$ printf 'Type: %s\n' "${ta#type:}"
Type: json
```

We can chop a string from the *end* of the value instead using % instead of #:

```
$ ta='type:json'
$ printf 'Field name: %s\n' "${ta%:*}"
Field name: type
```

Note that the stripped string can include **wildcards**: * to match any number of characters, or ? to match one. In the preceding example, we stripped :*, or the rightmost string following a colon.

If you want to trim a pattern with literal asterisks, you need to escape or quote them:

```
$ text='*WARNING'
$ printf '%s\n' "${text#\*}"
WARNING
$ printf '%s\n' "${text#'*'}"
WARNING
```

The preceding forms will will lean toward removing *smaller* occurrences of the pattern rather than larger ones. If you want to chop the longest possible match of a pattern with * in it, double the applicable sign: # becomes ##, and % becomes %%. The first is useful for stripping an entire leading path with */:

```
$ path=/usr/local/myscript/bin/myscript
$ printf 'Filename with path removed: %s\n' "${path##*/}"
Filename with path removed: myscript
```

Extracting substrings

If we know a specific substring we want to extract from a variable by where it starts, and optionally how long it is, we can use the ${var:start} or ${var:start:length} form:

```
bash$ title='== Password =='
bash$ printf '%s\n' "${title:3}"
Password ==
bash$ printf '%s\n' "${title:3:8}"
Password
```

By specifying a negative start value, you can start the counting from the *end* of the string, starting at −1:

```
bash$ alpha='abcdefghijk'
bash$ printf '%s\n' "${alpha: -3:2}"
ij
```

Note that we had to add a space prefix before the minus sign, to prevent the shell from interpreting this as the unrelated `:-` form.

Getting string length

The "`${#myvar}`" form can be used to expand to the length of a string:

```
bash$ alpha='abcdefghijk'
bash$ printf '%u\n' "${#alpha}"
11
```

While this form is Bash-specific, it's a short and convenient alternative to counting characters with `wc`. Note that it counts *characters* according to your locale, not bytes, and not screen columns either, so be cautious when counting characters outside the ASCII set. Some Japanese characters, for example, will expand to "1" with an `en_US.UTF-8` locale, even though they're 4 bytes long, and will usually take 2 screen columns.

Substituting strings

Substituting patterns in expansions can be done with the "`${myvar/pattern/replacement/}`" form:

```
bash$ promise='I'\''ll do it today.'
bash$ printf '%s\n' "${promise/today/tomorrow}"
```

This only replaces the *first* instance of the pattern. If you want to replace *all* instances of the pattern, use two slashes before the first pattern rather than just one:

```
bash$ promise='Yes, today. I'\''ll do it today.'
bash$ printf '%s\n' "${promise/today/tomorrow}"
Yes, tomorrow. I'll do it today.
bash$ printf '%s\n' "${promise//today/tomorrow}"
Yes, tomorrow. I'll do it tomorrow.
```

Note that the pattern being replaced uses the wildcard (globbing) syntax, with `*` matching multiple characters, and `?` matching only one; it is *not* a regular expression as might be used with `sed` or `awk`:

```
bash$ promise='Yes, today. I'\''ll do it today.'
bash$ printf '%s\n' "${promise/today*/I\'ll do it soon.}"
Yes, I'll do it soon.
```

Changing case

You can have a variable expand into its value with all characters uppercase or lowercase using the "${myvar^^}" and "${myvar,,}" forms, respectively:

```
bash$ fn='mixedCase'
bash$ printf '%s\n' "${fn^^}"
MIXEDCASE
bash$ printf '%s\n' "${fn,,}"
mixedcase
```

Can you guess what the form with a *single* ^ or , might do, rather than a double one? Try it out.

Combining parameter expansion forms

You cannot combine the preceding parameter expansion forms into one expansion; "${myvar:-foo#.ext}" does not do what you might hope. You could use a temporary variable instead, to run them one at a time:

```
#!/bin/bash
temp="${myvar:-foo}"
printf '%s\n' "${temp#.ext}"
```

Doing math in Bash

Bash supports simple integer (whole number) arithmetic operations with its **arithmetic expressions**. The syntax for expanding these is a set of *double parentheses* after the usual $ expansion sign:

```
$ num_a=3
$ num_b=2
$ printf 'The sum of the two numbers is: %u\n' "$((num_a + num_b))"
The sum of the two numbers is: 5
```

Notice in the preceding expression, `"$((num_a + num_b))"`, we did not have to use the `$` prefix to expand the `num_a` and `num_b` variables names. Assignments to other variables can be performed in the same way:

```
$ diff="$((num_a - num_b))"
$ printf 'The difference of the two numbers is: %u\n' "$diff"
The difference of the two numbers is: 1
```

We can do many different kinds of operations with these expressions, using both variables and literal numbers:

```
# Three raised to the power of two (squared)
$ printf '%u\n' "$((3**2))"
9
# 180 divided by 60
$ printf '%u\n' "$((180/60))"
3
# 1 or 0, depending on whether one number is greater than another
$ printf '%u\n' "$((2 > 1))"
1
$ printf '%u\n' "$((30 > 40))"
0
```

The full list of operations supported by these expressions is available after the "ARITHMETIC EVALUATION" in the Bash manual page. They are mostly taken from the C language, and the order in which the operations are evaluated is the same as in that language.

Fixed or floating-point arithmetic

If you try out a few of the preceding mathematical expressions, you might notice that some of the expanded values seem wrong:

```
$ printf '%.2f\n' "$((3/2))"
1.00
```

You may have expected a value such as `1.50` to be returned here, but Bash does not support floating-point or fixed-point arithmetic, only integer arithmetic. Fractional parts for these operations are lost.

If you need to perform arithmetic with non-integers using tools that are highly likely to be available on a POSIX system, your best bets are the bc calculator for fixed-point, or an AWK program for floating-point:

```
$ bc <<'EOF'
scale=2
3/2
EOF
1.50
$ awk 'BEGIN { printf "%.2f\n", 3/2 }'
1.50
```

If you have to do a lot of these sorts of operations, you should consider using a different programming language entirely. Bash is not the best language for heavy numerical analysis.

Using globs

A `*` unquoted asterisk character on a command line has a special meaning to Bash: it means it should expand the word in which the character occurs to all of the matching *filenames* if possible, but (by default) to leave the word unchanged if there are no such matching files.

This can be confusing, and is best explained with a few examples. Suppose our current directory has the following filenames:

```
$ ls -a
.  ..  .bashrc  april  august  october  september
```

A glob by itself will expand to all the filenames that are not prefixed with a dot:

```
$ printf '%s\n' *
april
august
october
september
```

Note that the filenames are expanded in alphabetical order – or, more correctly, the order specified by your language environment's **collation** settings.

If there are other letters in the same word as a glob, they have to match the relevant filenames in the same position. We could get all the filenames starting with a with a*:

```
$ printf '%s\n' a*
april
august
```

Or the filenames ending in ber with *ber:

```
$ printf '%s\n' *ber
october
september
```

Or both – we can put two globs on the same line, and they will be expanded in order:

```
$ printf '%s\n' a* *ber
april
august
october
september
```

Rather than matching *any number* of characters, we can also match a *single* character with a question mark, ?:

```
$ printf '%s\n' ????ber
october
```

Note that here, october was printed but september was not, because only october matched the condition: four characters – no more, no less – followed immediately by three characters, ber.

Rather than matching any character with ?, you can also define valid sets of characters with the [...] syntax:

```
$ printf '%s\n' *[lr]
april
october
september
```

The pattern used here could be read as "any filename ending with l or r." Note that august was not printed, as it does not match. These sets can be inverted with an exclamation mark as the first character in the range:

```
$ printf '%s\n' *[!lr]
august
```

Now the pattern matches anything that does *not* end with l or r.

For brevity, these ranges can also be represented with hyphenated ranges, or character classes. Full details on these ranges are available under the "Pathname Expansion" heading in the bash manual page:

```
[a-z]
[0-9]
[[:alnum:]]
```

Configuring globbing behavior

Bash offers a few options to change the way POSIX-specified globbing behavior works; two of the most useful are dotglob and nullglob.

Including dot files, but excluding dot and dot-dot

Note that .bashrc was not included in our example output. We might try to include it by prefixing a *second* glob with . – but this also includes the . and .. implied entires, referring to the current and parent directory. That could be a disaster if we were going to run rm -r:

```
$ printf '%s\n' * .*
april
august
october
september
.
..
.bashrc
```

We will almost never actually want this behavior. One POSIX-compatible way of working around it is using character globbing to exclude . and .. specifically, by requiring a second character that is not a dot:

```
$ printf '%s\n' * .[!.]*
april
august
october
september
.bashrc
```

But this would exclude a file named `..bashrc` with *two* leading dots, which – while unconventional – is still a valid filename. How frustrating! Bash offers an option to deal with this called `dotglob`, which includes dot files in glob expansion for `*`, but excludes the `.` and `..` implied entries:

```
$ shopt -s dotglob
$ printf '%s\n' *
.bashrc
april
august
october
september
```

Expanding to nothing

You may also have noticed with some experimentation with globs that if the pattern does not match anything, it expands to itself, unchanged:

```
$ printf '%s\n' c*
c*
```

Because none of our test files start with `c`, the glob is unexpanded and unchanged. This may seem strange; surely it would be better if the pattern expanded to nothing at all? It makes more sense when you consider the behavior of many classic Unix commands; if there are no arguments, they default to assuming input is coming from standard input. For example:

```
$ cat -- c*
cat: 'c*': No such file or directory
```

Because the pattern here did not expand, `cat` saw the `c*` argument, found the file named `c*` did not exist, and reported that to us, with an error message that gives us some idea of what went wrong.

Bash does allow us to alter this behavior; if we set the `nullglob` option, `c*` really will expand to nothing at all:

```
bash$ shopt -s nullglob
bash$ printf '%s\n' c*
bash$
```

However, note that if we then used the `c*` pattern on a `cat` command line, for example, and there were no matching files, it would simply stop, waiting for input from the terminal – probably not what you intended to happen:

```
bash$ shopt -s nullglob
bash$ cat -- c*
```

So `nullglob` can be a very useful option – but be careful when using it in scripts.

Case-insensitive globbing

Setting the Bash `shopt` option to `nocaseglob` allows us to make globs match case-insensitively:

```
bash$ shopt -s nocaseglob
bash$ printf '%s\n' A*
april
august
```

In this example, the lowercase `april` and `august` were matched and returned, even though the glob started with an uppercase `A`.

Extended globbing

Creative use of globbing syntax can do a great deal of advanced pattern matching, but in some cases we may need something more advanced, perhaps approaching regular expressions in terms of complexity. Bash's `extglob` feature allows us to do this. With this `shopt` option enabled, we can use some additional glob forms:

- `?(pattern)`: Match up to one occurrence of the pattern
- `*(pattern)`: Match any number of occurrences of the pattern
- `+(pattern)`: Match at least one occurrence of the pattern
- `@(pattern)`: Match exactly one occurrence of the pattern
- `!(pattern)`: Match everything except the pattern

For example, `/var/log/!(*.gz)` matches all files in `/var/log` that *don't* end in `.gz`.

Some of these are useful only when using multiple patterns separated by a pipe character, `|`; for example, `/var/log/@(sys|mess)*.gz` matches all compressed log files that start with either `sys` or `mess`.

This option can be useful, but don't use it if you can express what you need with a simple classic glob, or a set of them; we could have done the same as the previous example with `/var/log/sys*.gz /var/log/mess*.gz`, without needing the `extglob` option at all.

Using arrays

It's sometimes the case that we'd like to store a set of multiple values in one variable, where we don't know how many there might be at the time we start the program, especially sets of filenames. Unfortunately, it's not safe to store a set of filenames in a simple string variable, even when separated by newlines, because a newline is itself a valid character for filenames – there's no safe choice of **delimiter** for the data, because we can't use null bytes in shell words.

Fortunately, Bash provides **arrays** to allow us to do this:

```
bash$ fruits=('apple' 'banana' 'cherry')
```

 Arrays are not specified at all as part of POSIX shell. They are a feature specific to Bash.

Note that we separate the parts of the array only with *spaces*, not commas, and we do *not* quote the parentheses; they are part of the syntax. With this array defined, we can expand members of it with numeric suffixes in square brackets, starting from 0:

```
bash$ printf '%s\n' "${fruits[0]}"
apple
bash$ printf '%s\n' "${fruits[2]}"
cherry
```

We can reference values indexed from the *end* of the array with negative subscripts, starting with `-1`:

```
bash$ printf '%s\n' "${fruits[-1]}"
cherry
```

We can expand *all* of the array elements using @ as a special subscript value:

```
bash$ printf '%s\n' "${fruits[@]}"
apple
banana
cherry
```

We will be using arrays a great deal in the next chapter when discussing loops and conditionals.

One convenient property of arrays is that after expanding them with the special @ index, we can apply parameter expansion operations to every element:

```
bash$ printf '%s\n' "${fruits[@]^^}"
APPLE
BANANA
CHERRY
```

Glob expansion in arrays

Arrays are especially useful when used to contain expanded globs:

```
bash$ myhomefiles=("$HOME"/*)
bash$ printf '%s\n' "${myhomefiles[@]}"
/home/bashuser/code
/home/bashuser/docs
/home/bashuser/music
/home/bashuser/Important Notes.txt
/home/bashuser/**README**
```

The `myhomefiles` array defined here contains a list of all files and directories matched by the * glob in our home directory, and stores them safely, even if they contain special characters, such as spaces, asterisks, or even newlines.

If you wish to store arguments for a command to execute later or for a script to iterate through, you should always use arrays (or positional parameters with `set --`). Never try to separate the files out from a single variable afterwards, with spaces or newlines – it's neither reliable nor safe.

Associative arrays

Bash 4.0 also introduced associative arrays, allowing string indices for arrays rather than numeric offsets, rather like a dictionary in Python, or a hash in Perl:

```
bash$ declare -A myassocarray
bash$ myassocarray=([apple]="red" [banana]="yellow" [carrot]="orange")
bash$ printf '%s\n' "${myassocarray[banana]}"
yellow
```

Be careful to `declare` the array with `-A` first if you want to use this, otherwise Bash may treat the array and operations done with it using numeric indices.

We won't use associative arrays in the rest of this book – while useful for those who want a dictionary type for shell scripting, they're a relatively new addition to the language, well outside the specifications for shell scripting languages. A case could reasonably be made that the tasks that need them might be a better fit for languages such as AWK, Perl, or Python.

Summary

With a basic grasp of how to assign, expand, and manipulate variables, arrays, and pattern-matching in Bash, we're now in a position to use them in tests and loop structures to complete the basic features of Bash as a programming language, which we'll do in the next chapter.

6
Loops and Conditionals

In this chapter, we'll learn how to work with **conditionals** and then **loops** in Bash using the `if`, `for`, and `while` shell keywords. These allow us to execute commands *conditionally* and/or *repeatedly*, giving us **control flow** for our scripts.

We will cover:

- How to use the `if` keyword
- The use of and the difference between the `[` builtin and the `[[` keyword
- When to use Bash's `((` arithmetic compound command
- How to match values with the `case` keyword
- How shell script `for` loops work
- Using Bash's alternative C-style `for` loops
- Using `while` loops
- The `while read -r` idiom for reading data line by line
- Choosing between `for` and `while`

Shell script's syntax for these structures is somewhat unique, largely for historical reasons and to fit into its command-centered structure, and only partly resembles comparable features in other programming languages.

Using the if keyword

A shell script is fundamentally a sequence of commands. In such a script, we very often want to run a command only if a testable condition is true. In earlier chapters, we already saw one way to do this, with the `&&` **control operator**:

```
$ grep -q bash /etc/shells && printf 'Bash is a system shell\n'
```

The preceding command line separates two commands with `&&`. The second command, which prints a string to standard output, only runs if the first command, `grep -q bash /etc/shells`, finds the `bash` string in the `/etc/shells` file and hence exits with status zero (success).

Using the `if` keyword, we can make this conditional approach more flexible, and somewhat easier to read:

```
$ if grep -q bash /etc/shells ; then printf 'Bash is a system shell\n' ; fi
```

The preceding command line could also be written like this in script form:

```
if grep -q bash /etc/shells ; then
    printf 'Bash is a system shell\n'
fi
```

Don't forget the `then` keyword, with the `;` separator before it; both are required. If you prefer, you can put `then` on a new line after the test command instead.

> Note that the keyword at the end of the condition, `fi`, is just `if` backwards.

In shell script, what is expected after the `if` keyword is not an *expression*, but a *command* to run, the outcome of which determines whether the code between the `then` and `fi` keywords is run.

The command line tested by `if` can be any command, builtin or not. For example, you can execute commands only if an attempt to change the working directory with `cd` was successful:

```
if cd /usr/local ; then
    printf >&2 'Successfully changed directory\n'
fi
```

We can *reverse* the test using the `!` keyword before the command, separated by spaces:

```
if ! cd /usr/local/myscript ; then
    printf >&2 'Failed to changed directory\n'
    exit 1
fi
```

The `printf` command in this example would only run if the script's attempt to change the working directory to /usr/local/myscript *failed*. Coupled with an early `exit`, this can be an effective way to abort a script and prevent the rest of it from running if some essential condition can't be met.

There are also `elif` and `else` keywords for using after `if` to perform successive tests and specify alternatives if the initial command exits with failure:

```
if cd /usr/local/myscript ; then
    printf >&2 'Changed to primary directory'
elif cd /opt/myscript ; then
    printf >&2 'Changed to secondary directory'
else
    printf >&2 'Couldn'\''t find a directory!'
    exit 1
fi
```

The script will try to change its working directory to /opt/myscript *only* if its attempt to change it to /usr/local/myscript fails first. If *both* attempts fail, it will print an error message, and then exit with 1 (failure).

We can perform a lot of useful logic by testing commands once we know how their exit values work, but very often – perhaps *more* often – what we actually want is to test some sort of **conditional expression**, for example:

- Does a variable's value match a string?
- Is a variable empty?
- Is one number greater than another?
- Is a file empty?

There are dedicated commands that are designed to help us do all of this.

Using the test command

The POSIX standard for the shell scripting language specifies a command named `test` that can be used to test something, and return an exit status to reflect the result.

Which kind of expression to evaluate is specified with the arguments to `test`. A straightforward and useful test is string equality; are two strings the same? We can try this out with an equals sign between two other shell words:

```
$ myshell=bash
$ test "$myshell" = 'sh' && printf 'Match!\n'
```

```
$ test "$myshell" = 'bash' && printf 'Match!\n'
Match!
```

Note that the equals sign needs to be a separate word for the test arguments, with spaces before and after, unlike the variable assignment, where we cannot have spaces.

Many other tests are possible:

- test -e 'myfile': Whether a file or myfile directory exists
- test -n "$myvar": Whether a myvar variable is set and not empty
- test -d 'mydir': Whether a directory with the name mydir exists
- test -s 'myfile': Whether a file myfile file is not empty

You can see a complete list of these with help test. You are likely to refer to this particular help page many times during your career as a Bash programmer!

Using the [command

A better-known form of the test command is the [command. The primary difference between the two is that] must be the last argument to [. This makes it look very much like a special syntax for shell script, but it isn't; it's just another command:

```
$ [ "$myshell" = 'bash' ] && printf 'Match!\n'
```

Being a command, this syntax can be used after if, just like the grep and cd examples earlier in this chapter:

```
myshell=bash
if [ "$myshell" = 'bash' ] ; then
    printf 'Match!\n'
fi
```

This is all specified by POSIX. Note that we still had to *quote* our variable to prevent special characters in its value from causing unwanted glob or whitespace expansion.

Using the [[keyword

Bash provides its own improved version of the [command, doubling it to [[. It's actually a **shell keyword**, a special part of the Bash syntax, and not just a regular builtin command:

```
#!/bin/bash
myshell=bash
```

```
if [[ $myshell = 'bash' ]] ; then
    printf 'Match!\n'
fi
```

One advantage of the [[keyword over the [builtin is that less *quoting* is required. You may notice in the preceding example that $myshell is not in double quotes.

Unfortunately, this benefit does not apply to the *right-hand side* of the =, ==, !=, or =~ operations. If you're testing two variables for equality, for example, you will still need to quote the one to the right of the equals sign:

```
[[ $myshell = "$yourshell" ]]
```

If you find this too confusing (or imbalanced!), you can just double-quote variables on both sides, the same way you would with the [command; it doesn't do any harm:

```
[[ "$myshell" = "$yourshell" ]]
```

Most of the tests described in help test work the same way with [[, just as well as they do with [or test itself. However, there are a few other differences. The first is that equality or inequality testing on strings does glob matching:

```
[[ $myshell = b* ]]
```

Because the right side of this expression is *unquoted,* Bash will check whether the value of the myshell variable starts with b; the rest of it can be any other set of characters, or none at all.

The [[keyword also supports a new operator, =~, to test whether strings match **regular expressions**:

```
[[ $myshell =~ 'sh$' ]]
```

This will test whether the myshell variable's value ends with the letters sh, with $ being a regular expression metacharacter meaning "end of string."

Arithmetic conditions

The POSIX specification for the test and [commands includes a few arithmetic tests for integers:

- ["$a" -eq "$b"]: Equal
- ["$a" -ne "$b"]: Not equal
- ["$a" -lt "$b"]: Less than

- ["$a" -le "$b"]: Less than or equal to
- ["$a" -gt "$b"]: Greater than
- ["$a" -ge "$b"]: Greater than or equal to

> Be careful not to confuse -lt and -gt with < and >; the latter are **lexicographic** tests, to see whether strings sort after one another. For example, [2 \> 10] exits successfully, because the "10" string sorts after "2"!

Sometimes using these tests with expansion of arithmetic expressions can be unwieldy to write; for example, if we wanted to test whether the value of the bytes variable, divided by 1,000, was greater than the kbytes variable, we might write:

```
if [ "$((bytes / 1000))" -gt "$kbytes" ] ; then
    . . .
fi
```

Bash includes its own syntax for testing arithmetic expressions with ((– *without* a leading $ sign – including all the terms in one expression, which is somewhat easier to read and debug:

```
if ((bytes / 1000 > kbytes)) ; then
    . . .
fi
```

The double parentheses, ((...)), can contain any **arithmetic expression**, like we saw in Chapter 5, *Variables and Patterns*, and it is treated like a *command* – its exit value reflects the outcome of the expression. An outcome of 0 is treated as false and exits with status 1, and any other outcome is treated as true, and exits with status 0:

```
((2 > 0))    # True; exits 0
((a = 1))    # True; exits 0, and variable a is assigned the value 1
((0 > 3))    # False; exits 1
((0))        # False; exits 1
((a = 0))    # False; exits 1, and variable a is assigned value 0
```

These expressions are very powerful and somewhat easier to manipulate than their POSIX-standardized equivalents. Remember that all of the arithmetic operations use **integers** only – no fractional (fixed or floating point) numbers.

Switching with the case keyword

Bash's extension to string equality tests for pattern matching is useful, but it can sometimes be more convenient to use the older POSIX-specified `case` construct, which is shell script's analogue of the C `switch` statement.

The `case` statement allows us to run commands based on the outcome of matching a string against glob patterns. For example, to check whether the `command` variable matches `help`, we might do this:

```
case $command in
    help) printf 'Command help:\n...' ;;
esac
```

Note the following details of this syntax:

- You don't have to double-quote `$command` just after the `case` statement.
- The pattern to match has a closing `)`, but does not require an opening one.
- The closing keyword is `esac`, which is `case` spelled backwards, just as the closing keyword for `if` is `fi`.
- Each option is terminated with *two* semicolons.

We can add other options according to the same pattern:

```
case $command in
    help) printf 'Command help:\n...' ;;
    version) printf 'Command version: 0.1.0\n' ;;
esac
```

We can specify alternative values for any of these options for the same outcome by separating the patterns with a pipe character:

```
case $command in
    help|h|usage) printf 'Command help:\n...' ;;
esac
```

Perhaps most usefully, we can include glob-matching characters: `*`, `?`, and `[...]` to test for *partial* matches. This is a good way to have a "catch all" or default option if nothing else matches:

```
case $command in
    debug|verb*)
        printf 'Running in verbose mode.\n'
        verbose=1
        ;;
```

```
      *) printf 'Unknown command\n' ;;
  esac
```

Remember that only the *first* condition that matches will be run; the others will be ignored, as long as they're correctly separated with two semicolons, ; ; .

Looping over shell words with for

The `for` keyword is used to define code to run repeatedly over a list of shell words:

```
#!/bin/bash
for system in bsd linux macosx windows ; do
    printf '%s\n' "${system^^}"
done
```

The preceding code loops through the list of four items, assigning each one in turn to the `system` variable. The body of the loop prints the value of the `system` variable in all caps, for each **iteration** of the loop.

Note the following about the preceding syntax:

- The variable name goes just after `for`, and before `in`
- `do` is required and needs to be *after* the semicolon, to specify where the variable and list of words finishes
- The loop is closed with `done`, not `rof` as you might have expected from `fi` and `esac`
- The list of words can be blank; `for system in ; do ... ; done` is not a syntax error, it just does nothing

The assignment of the `system` variable in this loop is not "scoped" in any meaningful sense. If this variable had a value assigned before the loop started, it will be lost. After the loop finishes, it will remain assigned to the final item, in this case the "windows" string.

The `in` for `for` is only required if you want to specify a word list inline. Otherwise, the `for` loop defaults to the list of arguments to the current shell or function, that is, the **positional parameters**, expandable as `"$@"`. We can test this out by assigning the parameters for the current shell; an alternative (but not exactly equivalent) way to write this might be as follows:

```
set -- bsd linux macosx windows
for system ; do
    printf '%s\n' "${system^^}"
done
```

We could write the second line like this instead, if we wanted to be explicit:

```
for system in "$@" ; do
```

The `for` loop is hence the correct choice for iterating over an arbitrary number of arguments on which your script or function is running. It's also the correct choice for iterating over *arrays*, which we can think of as storage for an arbitrary number of shell words:

```
#!/bin/bash
systems=(bsd linux macosx windows)
for system in "${systems[@]}" ; do
    printf '%s\n' "${system^^}"
done
```

This uses the special array subscript of `@` that we discussed in our introduction to arrays at the end of `Chapter 5`, *Variables and Patterns*, expanding to *every* value in the array. Don't forget the all-important double quotes around the expansion, too: `"${systems[@]}"`, *never* `${systems[@]}`.

Skipping an iteration

You can use the `continue` keyword to skip the rest of the current iteration and start the next one, if there is any. For example, this code gets the size of every one of a set of directories, but it only runs `du` if the directory actually exists:

```
#!/bin/bash
dirs=(/bin /home /mnt /opt /usr)
for dir in "${dirs[@]}" ; do
    [[ -d $dir ]] || continue
    du -s -- "$dir"
done
```

The `continue` keyword skips to the next run of the loop if the directory does not exist. It uses the `||` control operator to do this; if you prefer, you could write it with a full `if` statement instead.

As well as testing for the general case of file existence or type, loop continuations such as this are a useful method for dealing with unexpanded glob patterns. Recall that with Bash's default settings, a glob pattern such as `*` will remain unexpanded if there are no matching files. This means that the glob can sometimes show up in unwanted places:

```
for tmp in /tmp/myapp/* ; do
    printf >&2 'Warning: file %s still exists\n' "$tmp"
done
```

If `/tmp/myapp` does not exist, or is empty, the preceding code will print:

```
Warning: file /tmp/myapp/* still exists
```

This is probably not what you wanted! We can handle the case of an unexpanded glob with a `continue` condition:

```
#!/bin/bash
for tmp in /tmp/myapp/* ; do
    [[ -e $tmp ]] || continue
    printf >&2 'Warning: file %s still exists\n' "$tmp"
done
```

This method skips any filename that does not actually exist, to handle the case of unexpanded globs. It works for multiple unexpanded globs in the same list, too.

You could also deal with this quirk using a `find` call instead, or with the `nullglob` option described in Chapter 5, *Variables and Patterns* .

Ending the loop

The `break` keyword anywhere within the `for` loop stops the loop processing, and resumes execution at the first command after the loop's `done` keyword. It doesn't just skip the *rest* of the current iterations; it stops the *current* one too.

For example, the following code loops through the arguments given to the script or function, and adds each one to an `opts` array if it starts with a dash, –, such as `-l` or `--help`:

```
#!/bin/bash
opts=()
for arg ; do
    case $arg in
        -*) opts+=($arg) ;;
    esac
done
```

If we want to add support for the `--` option termination string, to allow the user a way to specify where the options finish, we could add a case with `break`, like so:

```
case $arg in
    --) break ;;
    -*) opts+=($arg) ;;
esac
```

With this added, when the loop encounters the exact string `--` (two characters) as an argument, it will stop processing; the rest of the arguments will not be checked, even if they do begin with a dash.

We sometimes refer to the use of `continue` and `break` statements as *short-circuiting* a loop.

Misuse of for loops

In code samples on the internet and others' shell scripts, you will often find command substitution used with `for` to iterate over lines of output; this is especially common with commands such as `ls`, `cat`, and `grep`:

```
# Bad practice
for item in $(ls) ; do
    ...
done
for line in $(cat TODO.txt) ; do
    ...
done
for match in `grep username ~/accounts` ; do
    ...
done
```

You should never attempt to iterate over lines with `for` loops, as in the preceding examples. The primary reason for this is that other characters besides newlines can separate arguments – spaces, for example. Another is that in order for the preceding code to work, the command substitution has to be *unquoted*, meaning that characters such as * or ? in the output can wreak havoc.

There are workarounds for both of these problems that *partly* work, such as setting the `IFS` variable and the `-f` shell option, respectively, but there's no real need for them when `while read -r` loops work better "out of the box."

If you want to iterate over output from a file or the output of a command, always use a `while read -r` loop. Limit `for` to iterate over arguments or arrays, or the C-style for loop described in the next section.

Using Bash's C-style for loops

Bash extends the `for` keyword to provide functionality similar to the three-argument `for` loop used in C:

```
#!/bin/bash
for ((i = 1 ; i <= 10 ; i++)) ; do
    printf '%u\n' "$i"
done
```

The preceding code prints the numbers from 1 to 10, each terminated by a newline, by assigning each number to the `i` variable in turn and then printing it. When followed by an unquoted `((`, the meaning of `for` changes; it does not iterate over a list of words, but instead loops using the three semicolon-separated statements in the double parentheses like so:

- **The first expression is run before the loop starts**: We assign the `i` value to zero to start it off.
- **The second expression is the test used to determine whether the loop should continue or stop**: We test whether the value of `i` is less than `10`.
- **The third expression runs after each instance of the loop**: We add one to the value of `i`.

If you want to read the `help` topic for this feature, you will need to *quote* it: `help 'for (('`.

You will sometimes read shell scripts that use the non-standard `seq` tool to do something similar to this:

```
# Not recommended
for i in $(seq 1 10) ; do
    printf '%u\n' "$i"
done
```

If Bash is available on your system, the `for` loop is somewhat easier to read, affords greater control, and does not rely on the availability of `seq`.

Using while loops

The `while` loop runs a command repeatedly, running the commands in the body of the loop each time the test command succeeds, and terminating the loop as soon as the command fails.

We could write the loop that prints the numbers from 1 to 10 that we implemented with `for` in the previous section like so:

```
#!/bin/bash
((i = 1))
while ((i < 10)) ; do
    printf '%u\n' "$i"
    ((i++))
done
```

Note the similarity to the C-style `for` loop here, with the difference that the first expression, `i = 1`, and the third expression, `i++`, have been moved out into separate statements.

A `while` loop also behaves much like a `for` loop in terms of flow control: an iteration of the loop can be skipped with `continue`, and the whole loop can be terminated with `break`.

Infinite loops

An **infinite loop** can be written using the `true` builtin with a `while` statement:

```
while true ; do
    printf 'Infinite loop!\n'
    sleep 1
done
```

The preceding code will print the "Infinite loop!" string followed be a newline endlessly, waiting for a second after each print. You can press *Ctrl + C* to stop the loop. The loop will never terminate on its own, because the `true` builtin in Bash always exits with status 0 (success), by design.

You will sometimes see the colon builtin, `:`, used instead of `true`; the effect is the same. You may find `true` is easier to read.

An infinite loop may not seem very useful at first, especially given Bash is not an event-driven or functional language that might require an event loop. There are still situations where such a loop can be useful in shell script. One common use is as a quick **wrapper script**, to run a program again even if it crashes or exits; this is often used to keep a game server daemon process running:

```
while : ; do
    mygameserver --foreground
    sleep 1
done
```

The `:` builtin still has a `help` topic, despite its odd name! Try `help :`.

Reading data line by line

We mentioned earlier in this chapter that `for` loops are often misused to read data line by line from files, or from the output of command pipes. The correct way to do this is with a very common idiom for use with `while` loops: repeatedly running the `read` command, always with its `-r` flag.

Consider a file named `fcs`, with the names of four famous computer scientists, one on each line:

```
Ken Thompson
Dennis Ritchie
John McCarthy
Larry Wall
```

We'd like a program to print out this table, but also to print a link to the person's article on the English-language Wikipedia after each line. There is no dedicated UNIX tool to do this, so we will write our own in Bash.

We might implement a rough version something like this:

```
#!/bin/bash
while read -r name ; do
    printf '%s\n' "$name"
    printf 'https://en.wikipedia.org/wiki/%s\n' "${name// /_}"
done < fcs
```

There's quite a lot to take in there, so let's break it down.

The `while` loop's test command is `read -r name`. `read` is a builtin command that accepts a *line* from standard input, and saves its contents into one or more variables. In this case, we will save the entirety of each line into one variable, called `name`.

We use the `-r` option for `read` to stop it from treating backslashes in input specially, potentially misinterpreting data. We don't have any backslashes in this particular data, but it's still a good habit to get into.

The input source for the loop, the `fcs` file, is specified at the *end* of the loop, after `done`. Recall from `Chapter 4`, *Input, Output, and Redirection*, that a **compound command** can have redirections for input and output applied to it, just like a simple command. A `while` loop is a compound command. In this instance, we're specifying the standard *input* for the loop, and hence for each `read -r` command.

Within the loop, there are two `printf` statements. The first prints the name just as we read it. The second prints a link to the Wikipedia page, after substituting an underscore for every space using parameter expansion.

If we save the script in a file named `fcs-wiki.bash`, and run it with `bash fcs-wiki.bash` in the same directory as the `fcs` file, we can see the output we wanted:

```
$ bash fcs-wiki.bash
Ken Thompson
https://en.wikipedia.org/wiki/Ken_Thompson
Dennis Ritchie
https://en.wikipedia.org/wiki/Dennis_Ritchie
John McCarthy
https://en.wikipedia.org/wiki/John_McCarthy
Larry Wall
https://en.wikipedia.org/wiki/Larry_Wall
```

Field splitting

Suppose we wanted to print only the last name of each of our computer scientists. We could use the `read` command's built-in word splitting to do this, by specifying *two* variables after `-r`:

```
while read -r firstname lastname ; do
    printf '%s\n' "$lastname"
done < fcs
```

This yields the names we wanted:

```
Thompson
Ritchie
McCarthy
Wall
```

Because there is more than one variable name given, each line read is *split* at the first space or tab, and the line up to that point is saved into the `firstname` variable. Because `lastname` is the *last* variable on the line, the entire rest of the line—not only the last field—is saved into that.

Saving fields into arrays

Using the `-a` option to the `read` builtin, we can save the separated fields of a read line of input as an *array* variable, instead of a set of named string variables. This is particularly useful if we have a varying number of fields on each line:

```
$ cat animals-by-letter
alligator anteater armadillo
bee
caribou cat

elephant
```

Note that the fourth line in the preceding data is blank!

We can get an array of all the animals on each line, as separated by spaces, into an array named `animals` for each loop run, and then iterate over that array with a `for` loop; a loop within a loop:

```
#!/bin/bash
while read -r -a animals ; do
    for animal in "${animals[@]}" ; do
        printf '%s\n' "$animal"
```

```
    done
done < animals-by-letter
```

On running this code, we get a list of all of the animals, each terminated by a newline:

```
alligator
anteater
armadillo
bee
caribou
cat
elephant
```

Notice that the fourth line being empty meant that the `animals` array read for that line ended up *empty*, so the `for` loop never ran `printf` during that iteration of the `while` loop.

Choosing the splitting character

The `read` builtin checks a special variable named `IFS` – the Internal Field Separator – to decide where to split the line it reads. If this variable is unset, as it has been for our examples so far, it splits on groups of spaces and tabs.

If our data is separated by some other character, for example by colons in `/etc/passwd`, we can set `IFS` as an environment variable for `read` to influence its behavior. For example, to print every numeric user ID from the file without using `cut`, we could do this:

```
while IFS=: read -r user pass uid gid gecos home shell ; do
    printf '%s\n' "$uid"
done < /etc/passwd
```

Notice that the setting for `IFS` to the colon character, `:`, occurs just before the `read` command, and there is no control operator between them. Recall from Chapter 5, *Variables and Patterns*, that this sets `IFS` as an **environment variable** for the `read` command, and *only* for the `read` command.

The `IFS` variable affects other word-splitting behavior outside of `read` too, but this is not often needed, and is something best avoided for beginners. If you need to change `IFS`, do it using the environment variable prefix trick if you can, to avoid unwanted side-effects.

Disabling whitespace trimming

It's important to note that by default, read *ignores* spaces and tabs at the start and end of a line when reading fields into variables:

```
$ cat lines
Line one
    Line two
  Line three
$ while read -r line ; do printf '%s\n' "$line" ; done
Line one
Line two
Line three
done <lines
```

A lot of the time, this is what you want, but if you do actually want the line literally in one variable including any leading and trailing spaces or tabs, you need to set IFS to a blank value for the read command:

```
$ while IFS= read -r line ; do
printf '%s\n' "$line" ;
done <lines
Line one
    Line two
  Line three
```

This also suppresses the field-splitting completely, of course, so you can only read the whole line into one variable this way.

Reading process output

As a compound command, a while loop can also accept the output of another command as input, using a pipe. For example, to pass the output of who -T to the loop as input, to print only the terminal names for active users on the system, we might write:

```
who -T | while read -r username state terminal _ ; do
    printf '%s\n' "$terminal"
done
```

Avoiding subshell problems

When passing program output into a compound command with a pipe, there's a subtle pattern of problems, which can be very hard to figure out, to do with **subshells**.

Consider this simple loop, which is intended to count the lines of output from a call to `who`, and then print it:

```
((count = 0))
who | while read -r ; do
    ((count++))
done
printf '%u\n' "$count"
```

When run, however, this program always prints zero for the count! Most new shell programmers eventually run into this sort of particularly baffling problem.

Because each command after the first command in a pipeline runs in its own subshell environment—its own forked process—changes to variables *do not persist* after the pipeline is completed. This means that the `count` variable inside the `while` loop correctly counts the input lines, but that count is discarded when the subshell ends, and the value is back at zero!

When the data is saved to a temporary file first, however, and the `while` loop is passed that file as input, the `while` loop runs in the *same* process, not in a subshell, and so the line-counting works correctly:

```
who > who.out
while read -r ; do
    ((count++))
done < who.out
printf '%u\n' "$count"
```

There are a few ways to deal with this without having to involve (and clean up) a temporary file. First, we can use a compound command to include *all* of the code that needs to use the `count` variable as part of the same subshell:

```
who | {
    while read -r ; do
        ((count++))
    done
    printf '%u\n' "$count"
}
```

This method works even in non-Bash shells, but it can be unwieldy if the code inside the pipeline is extensive. An easier method specific to Bash is with **process substitution**:

```
while read -r ; do
    ((count++))
done < <(who)
printf '%u\n' "$count"
```

Note the < <(who) syntax at the very end of the loop. The first left angle bracket, <, is a standard input redirection, with which we're already familiar. The new syntax in <(who) runs the command inside the parentheses and expands to a temporary file handle or filename, managed internally by Bash, containing the command's output.

As an alternative, there is also the lastpipe option set with shopt, which makes the last command in a pipeline run in the current shell, not a subshell:

```
shopt -s lastpipe
((count = 0))
who | while read -r ; do
    ((count++))
done
printf '%u\n' "$count"
```

This works in a script, but we recommend you use process substitution instead, as it behaves reliably whether the script is executed or sourced into an interactive shell.

Avoiding input problems with ssh

Another vexing problem with reading lines in a while read -r loop is that sometimes certain commands inside the loop can themselves consume some of the data intended for the read builtin, and it may not be immediately clear what those commands are.

One such command is the ssh OpenSSH client, which by default reads all the standard input it can once started to pass it as commands to the target system, even if a command is specified on the command line. Consider this list of SSH hostnames:

```
$ cat hostnames
alpha.example.com.
beta.example.com.
gamma.example.com.
```

We want to read each hostname, and run the uptime command on it to get a quick overview of how long it's been up and its load average. However, this doesn't seem to work:

```
while read -r hostname ; do
    ssh -- "$hostname" uptime
done < hostnames
```

The first iteration of the loop runs fine, and after perhaps typing a password or passphrase, we see the uptime of `alpha.example.com.` – but then the loop stops, with no error message!

This is because `ssh` has read the remaining two lines of the `hostnames` file during the first loop iteration, after the first line was saved into the `hostname` variable by the `read` builtin. The `-n` switch to `ssh` suppresses this behavior, instructing it not to read any standard input:

```
while read -r hostname ; do
    ssh -n -- "$hostname" uptime
done < hostnames
```

The loop then runs three times, reading each host and printing the output of its `uptime` program after running it via SSH.

Any program that reads standard input without you expecting it to may potentially run into this problem. If you can't find a way to prevent the program from reading standard input with configuration or options, you can try directing `/dev/null` into it:

```
while read -r item ; do
    program </dev/null "$item"
done < items
```

Summary

We use `for` loops to iterate through arguments or through ranges of numbers, and we use `while` loops to test conditions in the same way as `if` for more generic looping purposes, especially in the form of the `while read -r` idiom for reading files or command output line by line. Along with the use of the variables and arithmetic expressions from Chapter 5, *Variables and Patterns*, and the input- and output-redirection techniques from Chapter 4 *Input, Output, and Redirection*, we now have the building blocks to make all kinds of useful scripts in Bash.

In the next chapter, we'll look at the specifics of defining your own commands and scripts using these skills.

Scripts, Functions, and Aliases 7

In the previous chapter, we explored some of the most important commands provided to you by the Bash shell and by a Unix system that implements the POSIX standard. These commands have many uses on their own, and they can additionally serve as the basis for making your own **custom commands**, to perform specific tasks that you need and remember them for convenience in the future.

This chapter explores three different types of custom commands that you can write to use in your Bash scripts or on the Bash command line:

- **Aliases**: Can expand a word into a command line string
- **Functions**: A way to write a command from a set of other commands, much more versatile than aliases
- **Scripts**: Take the form of programs in files on your system, and unlike aliases and functions, can be used outside of Bash

We'll look at each of these in turn, demonstrating them with some short examples, and discuss when you should use each type of command.

Aliases

Aliases are quick and simple ways to make one command stand for a whole command line, expressed as a string. They are perhaps the best-known way to customize behavior in the Bash shell, but they are also the least flexible.

Depending on your system, it's possible you already have an alias or two defined by your startup scripts. When the builtin `alias` command is entered with no arguments, it lists all of the aliases defined in the current Bash session.

For example, on a Debian GNU/Linux server, a new user might have the following alias defined:

```
bash$ alias
alias ls='ls --color=auto'
```

This is also evident from running the `type` command on `ls` with the `-a` switch, which informs us that the command used is an alias:

```
bash$ type -a ls
ls is aliased to `ls --color=auto'
ls is /bin/ls
```

The purpose of this `ls` alias is to add the `--color=auto` option to any call to `ls`. Adding an option like this to every call is a very common use for aliases. For GNU `ls`, the `--color=auto` option specifies that the entries in the output of `ls` can be written in color if the output is to a color terminal.

Note that because an alias for `ls` exists, when a user issues an `ls` command, Bash uses it in preference to the `/bin/ls` program of the same name, hence its position as first in the list. When the `ls` command *inside* the alias is run, however, Bash doesn't run the `ls` alias again—that would be an infinite loop! Instead, it looks to the next item in the list, and runs the `/bin/ls` program instead. This means that aliases can't run themselves, though they can run other aliases.

Defining new aliases

We can define our own aliases to get similar option-defining shortcuts. Suppose we've been typing `ls -l` a lot to get a full file listing of the current directory. Because we run it so often, we'd like a way to type it with fewer keystrokes. We can define an `ll` alias like this:

```
bash$ alias ll='ls -l'
```

The `ll` name is thereafter available as a command that will expand to run the full `ls -l` command instead:

```
bash$ type ll
ll is aliased to `ls -l'
```

```
bash$ ll
total 16
-rw-r--r-- 1 bashuser bashuser 3526 Jul 15 16:42 .bashrc
-rw-r--r-- 1 bashuser bashuser  675 Jul 15 16:42 .profile
```

We can add further options to our call to the `ll` alias, such as specifying a file on which the command should run, in this case `.bashrc`:

```
bash$ ll .bashrc
-rw-r--r-- 1 bashuser bashuser 3526 Jul 15 16:42 .bashrc
```

We can verify this by briefly turning on the `-x` option for the shell, which will print the expanded command before executing it, after a + prefix:

```
bash$ set -x
bash$ ll .bashrc
+ ls -l .bashrc
-rw-r--r-- 1 bashuser bashuser 3526 Jul 15 16:42 .bashrc
bash$ set +x
```

Understanding shortcomings with aliases

Aliases are simple to understand, but they have some shortcomings as a means of writing your own commands. One of the biggest problems is that they have no way of modifying their behavior based on any arguments given to them; they are just simple text substitutions.

For example, suppose you wanted to make an alias, `mkcd`, that created a directory before changing into it—a very useful shortcut! If you wanted to do this with aliases, you might try to define it like this, separating each command with a semicolon:

```
bash$ alias mkcd='mkdir -p;cd'
```

But this doesn't work:

```
bash$ mkcd createme
mkdir: missing operand
Try 'mkdir --help' for more information.
-bash: cd: createme: No such file or directory
```

If we use `set -x` again, we can see the actual command Bash ran, and see what went wrong:

```
bash$ set -x
bash$ mkcd createme
```

```
+ mkdir -p
mkdir: missing operand
Try 'mkdir --help' for more information.
+ cd createme
bash: cd: createme: No such file or directory
bash$ set +x
```

The `createme` argument was only passed to the last command, `cd`; what Bash saw and executed was `mkdir -p; cd createme`. We need a way to pass the same argument to *both* commands. This attempt using `$1` to get the first argument doesn't work either:

```
bash$ alias mkcd='mkdir -p -- "$1" && cd -- "$1"'
bash$ mkcd createme
mkdir: cannot create directory '': No such file or directory
-bash: cd: too many arguments
```

With aliases, there is no practical way to handle this simple requirement. Functions *can* do this, however.

Another problem with aliases is that invoking them in Bash scripts doesn't work; they are strictly for use in interactive mode. Worse, there is no error raised when they're defined—they just don't work when called, so it's hard to tell what went wrong:

```
bash$ cat alias.bash
alias ll='ls -l'
ll
bash$ bash alias.bash
line 2: ll: command not found
```

To make it even more complicated, in some other shells, aliases *do* work in scripts. It's better to avoid the whole mess by always using functions instead, which work the same way in all POSIX family shells.

A third problem is that because the commands are in strings, escaping the characters or using quotes in the command definitions can get very confusing:

```
bash$ alias mybook='cd ~/'\''User'\''s Guide'\'
```

To summarize, our advice is to avoid aliases; they have no practical advantages over functions or scripts. The preceding discussion will help you edit aliases in other people's scripts that you may have to maintain—but if you can replace them with functions, do it! You will thank yourself later. Even the `bash` manual itself agrees:

> *For almost every purpose, aliases are superseded by shell functions.*

Functions

Functions are a much better way of defining your own commands for use on the Bash command line, and in Bash scripts. They can do everything aliases can, and more.

Well, almost everything. There are some niche tricks you can do with aliases and not functions alone, but they are essentially clever hacks and mostly a curiosity. Take a look at Simon Tatham's *Magic Aliases* article to learn more: `https://www.chiark.greenend.org.uk/~sgtatham/aliases.html`.

A great deal of what we discuss for functions will be applicable to the next section on scripts. There are some important differences in the way the two work, but they have a lot in common. We will highlight the similarities in the next section.

Defining functions

We can define a function as a new **name** given to a saved **compound command**, which is run each time a command of that name is called. That definition is somewhat dense, so we'll break it down with some examples.

A simple function definition in one line to print our home directory might take the following form:

```
bash$ home() { printf '%s\n' "$HOME" ; }
```

This definition has a few parts:

- A function **name**, followed by a pair of parentheses. The name must start with a letter, and the rest of the name must be only letters, numbers, or underscores. Bash allows a space before the parentheses, if you like. In this case, our function is named `home`.
- An opening **curly bracket**, to open the **compound command** that forms the body of the function. This must be followed by a space.
- At least one command, each one followed by a **control operator**, in this case a semicolon, to run the command and pause execution until it completes. If you leave the control operator out, you'll get a syntax error. A newline counts as a control operator.
- A closing **curly bracket** to complete the compound command.

You might have seen the `function` keyword used as an alternative way to declare functions, such as `function mkcd { ... }`. We recommend the `mkcd() { ... }` syntax instead, as it's consistent between shells.

After the preceding function is defined in an interactive shell, it can be run with the `home` command, and Bash's `type` builtin reports the `home` name as referring to a function:

```
bash$ home
/home/bashuser
bash$ type home
home is a function
home ()
{
    printf '%s\n' "$HOME"
}
```

Passing arguments to functions

If we try to implement our `mkcd` alias attempt from the previous section in functions, we meet with more success than our attempt with aliases. Here's one possible implementation:

```
bash$ mkcd() { mkdir -p -- "$1" && cd -- "$1" ; }
```

This function works as we wanted, ensuring the directory is created before we try to change into it:

```
bash$ pwd
/home/bashuser
bash$ mkcd createme
bash$ pwd
/home/bashuser/createme
```

Note that this `mkcd` function runs more than one command in its body: a `mkdir` call, and a `cd` call. It also includes the `"$1"` string, which expands to the value of the first **positional parameter** passed to the function. We can see this in action with `set -x`:

```
bash$ set -x
bash$ mkcd createme
+ mkcd createme
+ mkdir -p -- createme
+ cd -- createme
bash$ set +x
```

We separate mkdir and cd with &&, because we only want to change into the directory if it was successfully created: that is, we run the cd command only if the mkdir command exited successfully.

Note also how the argument we provided to mkcd, the createme directory name, was passed to both the mkdir command and to the cd command afterward, each time via the "$1" parameter.

Finally, note that we put $1 in double quotes to stop any special characters in its value being interpreted by Bash, per the discussion of quoting behavior in Chapter 2, *Bash Command Structure*. This allows us to apply mkcd to any directory name we want:

```
bash$ mkcd 'My Book'
bash$ mkcd '!@#$%^&*()'
bash$ mkcd \'
```

 You would hopefully never actually name a directory with just a literal apostrophe ('), but Bash lets you, if you want to, and your users might do so too. Your functions and scripts should anticipate any valid filenames they might wish to use.

After "$1", we can get the second positional parameter with "$2", the third with "$3", and so on. This can go beyond "$9" if you want, with curly brackets: "${10}", "${11}", and so on, but you should not need to index arguments that far very often.

Using -- to separate options from filenames

In our mkcd example, we preceded both calls to "$1" with a double dash, --, the **option terminator** string. This syntax specifies a point beyond which further arguments are meant as argument strings for the program, often filenames, and *not* as options, even if they start with hyphens, such as -dirname-.

This is so that the mkdir and cd commands know that whatever we pass in as $1 is *not* an option to the command, such as -p or --version, but a directory name on which to operate. Most commands that accept options use this syntax to separate options from filenames or other words, including bash itself:

```
bash$ bash --version
GNU bash, version 4.4.23(1)-release (x86_64-pc-linux-gnu)
bash$ bash -- --version
bash: --version: No such file or directory
```

If this seems unnecessary or overly cautious to you, try leaving out both of the -- strings when you define the function, and then running it with a new directory name such as --parent or -virtual:

```
bash$ mkcd --parent
mkdir: missing operand
Try 'mkdir --help' for more information.
bash$ mkcd -virtual
mkdir: invalid option -- 'i'
Try 'mkdir --help' for more information.
```

Imagine how hard it would be for someone else using your function to see these error messages, and to try to figure out what they did wrong!

Getting all the arguments

We could adapt our preceding mkcd function to a new function, mkls, that creates directories and then prints them with ls -dl. The -d option to ls lists the directory itself, rather than its content. This implementation works well:

```
bash$ mkls() { mkdir -- "$1" && ls -dl -- "$1" ; }
bash$ mkls newdir
drwxr-xr-x 2 bashuser bashuser 4 2018-07-17 20:30:33 newdir/
```

However, this approach only allows us to create *one* directory. Because both mkdir and ls accept more than one directory name, we could create two of them like this:

```
bash$ mkls2() { mkdir -- "$1" "$2" && ls -dl -- "$1" "$2" ; }
bash$ mkls2 newdir1 newdir2
drwxr-xr-x 2 tom tom 4 2018-07-17 20:32:03 newdir1/
drwxr-xr-x 2 tom tom 4 2018-07-17 20:32:03 newdir2/
```

But that means the function no longer works correctly for only *one* directory, presenting an error:

```
bash$ mkls2 singledir
drwxr-xr-x 2 bashuser bashuser 4 2018-07-17 20:30:33 singledir/
mkdir: cannot create directory '': No such file or directory
```

It would be convenient to get *all* of the function's arguments within the function, no matter how many there were. Fortunately, Bash has a syntax for this, with the special "$@" expansion parameter:

```
bash$ mkls() { mkdir -- "$@" && ls -dl -- "$@" ; }
bash$ mkls dirset1 dirset2 dirset3
```

```
drwxr-xr-x 2 bashuser bashuser 4 2018-07-17 20:38:01 dirset1/
drwxr-xr-x 2 bashuser bashuser 4 2018-07-17 20:38:01 dirset2/
drwxr-xr-x 2 bashuser bashuser 4 2018-07-17 20:38:01 dirset3/
```

"`$@`" expands to *all* of the arguments given to the function, *separately* quoted. You can also check this for yourself by changing the shell's own positional parameters with calls to `set` and `printf`:

```
bash$ set -- arg1 'argument 2' '-third argument'
bash$ printf '%s\n' "$@"
arg1
argument 2
-third argument
```

The double quotes around `$@` are just as important as they are around any other kind of variable or parameter expansion. Without them, special characters in the arguments might be interpreted by the shell, and may be broken up in a way you did not expect. You will never need an unquoted `$@` for original, practical Bash scripts.

Returning values from functions

Like filesystem scripts or programs, Bash functions can have **exit values**. These are integer values normally used to describe how well the function did its job, often for use by the calling shell or program to decide what to do next after the function completes. In the case of functions, we will call these **return values** for clarity, as they use the `return` keyword rather than `exit`.

Here's an example of a simple pair of functions, `succeed` and `fail`; rather like `true` and `false`, they always return 0 and 1, respectively:

```
bash$ succeed() { return 0 ; }
bash$ fail() { return 1 ; }
```

As observed in `Chapter 2`, *Bash Command Structure*, we can test these using the special `$?` parameter:

```
bash$ succeed;echo $?
0
bash$ fail;echo $?
1
```

A function does not have to have a `return` statement. If you leave it out, or use `return` without specifying a number afterward, the function's return value will be the exit value of the last command it ran. This means we could write `succeed()` and `fail()` like this instead, using the `true` and `false` commands:

```
bash$ succeed() { true ; }
bash$ fail() { false ; }
```

Be careful not to confuse `return` and `exit`. The former is for *functions*; the latter is for *scripts*. If you use `exit` in a function, the shell itself will exit, not just the function. This can be an unpleasant surprise when you're in the middle of some work!

An early `return` can sometimes be a good way to stop processing a function due to usage errors. This is sometimes referred to as **short-circuiting**. In our `mkcd` example, we know we can't accept more than one argument, because we can't change into more than one directory. We could add a few lines to the function for a full definition, like so:

```
mkcd() {
    if (($# != 1)) ; then
        printf >&2 'Need exactly one argument\n'
        return 1
    fi
    mkdir -- "$1" && cd -- "$1"
}
```

In this example, the function tests whether `$#` (the number of arguments) is equal to 1 before proceeding. If it's not exactly 1, the function prints an error message and returns 1, to represent having failed to do what it was asked, and the `mkdir` and `cd` commands are never run.

Understanding function input and output

It's important to note from the discussion on return values that *you cannot return strings or arrays from functions*. The `return` keyword is not used in the same way as in structured programming languages, such as PHP or JavaScript. It is strictly for integers, and it's intended to describe the function's *success or failure*, and not any product of its work.

Instead, for values calculated by a function, you should have the function print the *output* that you want, and use it in suitable ways in scripts. Using our home example function, the following code uses **command substitution** to include the function's output in a message of its own:

```
bash$ home() { printf '%s\n' "$HOME" ; }
bash$ printf '%s\n' "Your home directory is: $(home)"
Your home directory is: /home/bashuser
```

You can treat function calls that emit output on the command line or in scripts the same way you can any other command that emits output; the shell does not treat them specially in this regard. For example, we could count the number of characters in our home output with wc, like so:

```
bash$ home | wc -c
15
```

Note that in this example, wc still counted the newline character we printed at the end of the directory name, hence the count of 15 and not 14.

Similarly, functions can read data from standard *input* as well. Suppose we write a grep_un function that uses the grep command to search for any line that contains the current user's username:

```
bash$ grep_un() { grep -F -- "$USER" ; }
```

If we feed input into this function from a pipe while running as bashuser, it will behave as if grep bashuser were running on that input:

```
bash$ getent passwd | grep_un
bashuser:x:1003:1003:Bash User,,,:/home/bashuser:/bin/bash
```

Function scope

Functions defined during a bash session are only available *in that session*. You cannot define a function on the command line, and then expect to have it available in a Bash script you execute, or in another user's bash session. You would need to include the function definition in the script, and have the other user load your function first.

Functions that use curly brackets, { . . . }, for the function body operate in the current process of the shell. This allows you to have functions that can change your current working directory, such as cd shortcuts, to view and set variables for the current active shell, or to set shell runtime options, such as -x.

This means that variable assignments aren't local to functions; they're visible outside it, after the function has run:

```
bash$ func1() { foo=bar ; printf '%s\n' "$foo" ; }
bash$ func1
foo
bash$ declare -p foo
declare -- foo="bar"
```

If you want to set variables that are only visible inside the function body, you can use the local Bash keyword to declare the variable as being local to the function before you set it:

```
bash$ func2() { local baz ; baz=quux ; printf '%s\n' "$baz" ; }
bash$ func2
quux
bash$ declare -p baz
-bash: declare: baz: not found
```

 Note that local variables and the local keyword are not defined by POSIX; they're only guaranteed to work in Bash.

If you want to run a function so that it doesn't affect your current shell at all, including shell options, positional parameters, and current working directory, one method is to run it with a **subshell body** instead, by using parentheses instead of curly brackets. Consider these two functions, etc1 and etc2:

```
bash$ etc1() { cd /etc ; }
bash$ etc2() ( cd /etc )
```

Notice that the function body for etc2 is surrounded with parentheses and not curly brackets. Also note that for this function type, a control character such as ; is not required after the last command.

If we run each of these functions, we can see that the first one changes the current directory of our shell, but the second one does not:

```
bash$ cd ~
bash$ etc1
```

```
bash$ pwd
/etc
bash$ cd ~
bash$ etc2
bash$ pwd
/home/bashuser
```

This is because the directory change in the `etc2` function took place in a subshell; its parent process, our interactive shell, did not have its own working directory changed.

Reloading functions at shell startup

We can declare as many functions on the Bash interactive shell as we like, but just as functions are only visible during that `bash` session, they're not persistent either: as soon as the Bash shell in which they were declared exits, they disappear.

If you write a function on the command line that's convenient for you and that you'd like to be available in future sessions, you might want to arrange for that function to be loaded on startup. For most Bash configurations, a good place to put such function declarations is in your `~/.bashrc` file. On many systems, such a file may already exist, provided for you with some starting configuration and aliases.

Fortunately, Bash makes it easy to save defined functions for later use; you can reproduce code that will declare them with the `-f` option of `declare`. Let's examine the output of this command when run with our `home` example function:

```
bash$ declare -f home
home ()
{
    printf '%s\n' "$HOME"
}
```

Note that the function doesn't resemble exactly how we declared it, which was all on one line; this is how `bash` has chosen to format it, but it still works the same way. We can save this into our `~/.bashrc` file for later, using >> so that we append to the file's existing contents, rather than >, which would overwrite it:

```
bash$ declare -f home >> ~/.bashrc
```

If you examine the `~/.bashrc` file in your favorite editor, you'll find that the function declaration is now at the end of it. If the `.bashrc` file is indeed being sourced on startup for interactive shells as normal, then the function will be available to you the next time you start an interactive bash session on the same host and as the same user.

If you change your ~/.bashrc file, you can also reload it without logging out by typing source .bashrc.

Scripts

The third method of creating your own commands with Bash is to put them in a **script**: a file that you can arrange for bash to interpret and execute from the filesystem by name.

What a "script" means to Bash can mean many different things depending on context. In this book, we'll focus on scripts stored as executable program files on our filesystem, external to the Bash process itself.

Scripting methods

There are three general ways to run a script file in Bash: sourcing it, providing it to bash as input, and as a standalone script. For the following examples, we'll use the hello.bash script, with the following contents:

```
printf 'Hello, %s!\n' "$USER"
```

Sourcing the script means to use the Bash source command to read all of the commands in a script into the current shell session and run them there. A source command to read in a script such as hello.bash might look like this:

```
bash$ source hello.bash
Hello, bashuser!
```

This method behaves rather like a function, in that it runs the commands as if you had entered them from your own shell. Variable settings, directory changes, shell options, and other changes will apply to the current running shell session. This may not necessarily be what you want—more often than not, you will want the script to do its work, and then exit and leave you back at your shell session without changing any of your settings.

To avoid this, we can also provide the script to bash explicitly as *input*. You can either call the bash program with the script name as an argument, or provide it as input with a pipe or redirection:

```
bash$ bash hello.bash
Hello, bashuser!
```

```
bash$ cat hello.bash | bash
Hello, bashuser!
bash$ bash < hello.bash
Hello, bashuser!
```

This starts a new Bash **subprocess**, which runs the commands in the file, and then exits.

However, this method requires us to know that bash is the interpreter for the program, and means the command has at least two parts. Someone else using our script may not care what language it works in; they just want to run it! It would therefore be convenient to be able to just run the script directly, using only its name, which the next section explains.

Writing a shebang script

We can accomplish a self-executing script with a special syntax, #!, called a **shebang**, or sometimes **hash-bang**, as the first line of the script. This syntax is treated specially by the kernel, and specifies the program that should be used to run the rest of the script—the **interpreter**.

We edit hello.bash to put the shebang as the very first line of the script:

```
#!/bin/bash
printf 'Hello, %s!\n' "$USER"
```

The preceding syntax assumes that your Bash shell is in the common location of /bin/bash. You can find out where yours is by checking the value of the BASH variable:

```
bash$ declare -p BASH
declare -p BASH="/usr/local/bin/bash"
```

We also need to use the chmod system program to make the script executable:

```
bash$ chmod +x hello.bash
```

This sets the **executable bit** for all users of the script, allowing it to be executed directly as its own program, without needing to specify bash on the command line:

```
bash$ ./hello.bash
Hello, bashuser!
```

Now that the script knows its own interpreter, we don't need the `.bash` extension anymore, so we can use `mv` to rename the program to just `hello`:

```
bash$ mv hello.bash hello
bash$ ./hello
Hello, bashuser!
```

This has the effect of making our script into a program that knows how to run itself, and instructs the kernel on what to do when a user executes it. The user of our program is able to run it without needing to think about what language the program is written in. We can even release a new version later with the same name and that does the same thing, but written in an entirely different language!

It's very likely that many of your most-used programs on a GNU/Linux or other Unixlike system are in fact scripts with shebang lines—not compiled from languages such as C, but *scripts*, interpreted each time you run them. The `file` tool can help you identify them; for example, the `ldd` program on Debian GNU/Linux turns out to be a Bash script:

```
bash$ file /usr/bin/ldd
Bourne-Again shell script, ASCII text executable
```

Finding scripts with $PATH

You may have noticed in the previous section that we haven't yet called `hello` in quite the same way we would another program; we still have to put the `./` prefix first, or specify a full path to it. It doesn't work otherwise:

```
bash$ ./hello
Hello, bashuser!
bash$ /home/bashuser/hello
Hello, bashuser!
bash$ hello
bash: hello: command not found
```

What's missing? The answer is that we need to use the special `PATH` variable to specify where it can find commands such as `hello`, without needing to specify a full filesystem path to them.

Let's take a look at the value of `PATH`; your own value may vary:

```
bash$ declare -p PATH
declare -x PATH="/usr/local/bin:/usr/bin:/bin"
```

We notice two things:

- It's an **environment variable** (-x); that means the variable name and its value is passed down through child processes. Any programs we run will get a copy of the PATH variable as it was when we called the program.
- It's a **colon-separated** list of **directories**, most or all of which end in bin or sbin.

Each of the directories specified in the value of the PATH variable are locations to be searched, in order, for any given program that the user requests be run. The first matching command found is run, and the rest are ignored. We will call these **bindirs**, short for **logical binary directories**.

> Directories in PATH are only searched for a program if a builtin, alias, or function by the requested name doesn't exist; those command types always take priority. That's why you can't replace echo by making a new program called /usr/local/bin/echo.

So, in order to run hello from anywhere on the system without having to specify its full path, we need to put it in one of the directories in that variable. Which one should we pick?

System bindir

A typical location for programs that are accessible system-wide on most Unix-like systems is /usr/local/bin, and this directory is included in the $PATH of every user. If you want hello to be available system-wide, and you have permission to write to /usr/local/bin, you might put it there, using su or sudo to get root permissions first:

```
bash$ sudo -s
Password:
bash# mv hello /usr/local/bin
```

Note that for the last command line, we use bash# instead of bash$, to denote a shell that is running as the system administrative root user.

If we're able to do this, we should be able to call the hello program from anywhere on the system and as any user, just with the word hello:

```
bash$ hello
Hello, bashuser!
bash$ sudo -s
Password:
bash# hello
Hello, root!
```

User bindir

If we don't have root access, or we only want our script to be accessible to us, the other approach to getting our program in a PATH directory is to *make our own* bindir.

This can be any directory you like. The system does not require bin to be the name of the directory, but it's a good idea because it will make clear what the directory is for. We'll create a new user bindir in our home directory, called ~/bin.

First, we create the directory with mkdir, and then put hello inside it:

```
bash$ mkdir /home/bashuser/bin
bash$ mv hello /home/bashuser/bin
```

If we try running hello now, it still doesn't work, because our new bindir is not yet part of PATH. We can do that by adding the directory to the end of PATH with a variable assignment:

```
bash$ PATH=$PATH:/home/bashuser/bin
```

With this done, our command now works:

```
bash$ hello
Hello, bashuser!
```

We can make sure Bash is running the command we expected with a few type checks:

```
bash$ type -a hello
hello is /home/bashuser/bin/hello
bash$ type -t hello
file
bash$ type -p hello
/home/bashuser/bin/hello
```

This shows us that the hello *file* in our new user bindir is definitely being run when we invoke the hello command. We hope that by now you can see how useful the type command is for understanding what commands are actually doing on your system.

If we want to keep this setup permanently, we will need to make sure that our new directory is added to PATH each time we log in. You can do this by adding a line to your .bash_profile file, or .profile if .bash_profile does not exist:

```
PATH=$PATH:/home/bashuser/bin
```

This will append our `/home/bashuser/bin` bindir to the end of the existing value of `PATH` on every login, so that any scripts we put in our user `bindir` will be available to us by any process we run—not just Bash!

Arguments to scripts

Arguments to scripts work in exactly the same way they do for functions:

- You can get the arguments as positional parameters with `"$1"`, `"$2"`, `"$3"`, and so on
- You can dynamically get all of the positional parameters without having to count them with `"$@"`
- You can *count* the number of positional parameters if you need to with `"$#"`

Understanding sh vs bash

If you have worked with shell script before, you might be wondering why we used `#!/bin/bash` as our shebang in all our examples, and not `#!/bin/sh`. Many users think that the `/bin/sh` and `/bin/bash` programs work the same way as shell script interpreters on every system. This is not true – there are important differences between the two.

The most important difference is that `/bin/sh` may not even be the same program as `/bin/bash`, and may therefore lack many of the programming features Bash adds that are not specified by the POSIX standard. Some GNU/Linux systems use `bash` as their `/bin/sh` implementation (Arch Linux, CentOS), but others do not (Debian GNU/Linux, Ubuntu).

When Bash is called as `sh`, it changes its behavior slightly to be consistent with the way the `/bin/sh` program is expected to work. However, most of its special features, such as the advanced `[[` syntax, still work even in this mode. This means that a script with `#!/bin/sh` as the interpreter that uses Bash features might work on one system, and not another. This can even change over time: if your system of choice changes its `/bin/sh` implementation from Bash to another shell, as Debian GNU/Linux did, your script may stop working correctly after an upgrade where it appeared to be working fine before.

If you're writing a Bash script, *use a* `bash` *shebang*. This makes clear to both the system and to anyone reading your script what shell it should run in. If you use `/bin/sh` while using non-POSIX features, the system may get it wrong, and the user will have to guess.

Using env

Another problem with porting Bash scripts is that Bash is not always reliably in the same location. On GNU/Linux systems, it's almost always available in /bin/bash. On other systems, such as FreeBSD, it might instead be in /usr/local/bin/bash.

One way of working around this portability problem is to use a trick with the /usr/bin/env program; using it as a shebang with bash as the argument will find the first bash program in PATH:

```
#!/usr/bin/env bash
```

This works well on *most* systems, but it's not perfect. One subtle problem with it is that it means the bash executable to run the script is chosen at runtime. This means that a user with their own copy of bash installed or with a PATH that points to a different version of bash might experience different behavior from the same script.

If you are distributing your script for other systems in an archive or in a system package, if at all possible, you should specify a fixed path, such as #!/bin/bash, for the correct interpreter either in the packaging process or at build time. For casual sharing of programs, using /usr/bin/env might be good enough, and even if it does not work, your users will be able to see the language you mean the script should run in, and can correct it to point to the right location of the bash program for their system.

Choosing between functions and scripts

Having established the difference between functions and scripts, how can we know which is the best to use in which situation?

The choice can be subtle, but here's a basic guide to start:

- If you want your command only to be limited to an interactive shell, for example to override interactive behavior, add options to a command, or other shortcuts, *use a function*. Filesystem programs are useable outside the Bash shell, while functions are limited to the Bash process only.
- If you want your command to affect a running shell process, such as to change your current shell directory, or to read or set shell variables, *use a function*. Filesystem programs cannot change properties of your current shell process.
- In all other situations, *use a script* as a filesystem program in a bindir specified in $PATH. This script will then be callable by the system in any other situation you need, not just in Bash.

Using functions in scripts

Functions can be defined and used in scripts, and it can be a good idea to do so. One common use is a `die` function that catches error conditions, prints any given messages, and then exits the script:

```
die() {
    printf >&2 '%s\n' "$@"
    exit 1
}
tempfile=$(mktemp) || die 'Could not create temporary file'
(( $# > 0 )) || die 'Need at least one argument'
[[ $1 != *:* ]] || die 'Colon not allowed in directory name'
```

Note that you have to declare the functions before you call them. It's best to put the functions near the top of the script.

Summary

We've seen how to use and write aliases, functions, and scripts, and demonstrated why you should almost always choose functions or scripts over aliases, including a demonstration of how to pass arguments for both to the commands within them.

Knowing how to implement your own custom commands effectively allows you to take full advantage of the expressiveness of the GNU Bourne-Again Shell. It's like extending the programming language by defining your own words for it, whether for your own private use, or to share with other users of the system. When you get good at doing this, and define many commands to suit your specific tasks, you can work so quickly and effectively that it looks like magic to anyone watching.

In the final, chapter, we'll go through some best practices for shell scripting—some general recommendations and techniques to make your scripts and functions safer, more correct, and more robust.

8
Best Practices

In this final chapter, we'll look at some techniques for programming in Bash defensively, safely, and productively, in a way that makes working with shell scripts a joy rather than a chore, especially by avoiding some nasty pitfalls in the language.

We'll revisit the following material from earlier chapters in more depth:

- Quoting correctly
- Handling filenames starting with dashes
- Separating output and diagnostics

We'll also cover:

- Keeping scripts brief and simple
- Keeping scripts flexible
- Respecting and applying the user's configuration
- Allowing scripts to run without user input
- Limiting the scope of shell state changes
- Avoiding path anti-patterns
- Avoiding Bash for untrusted user input
- Documenting scripts
- Using temporary files cleanly
- Cleaning up after a script
- A tool to check shell scripts for problems

Quoting correctly

It can't be over-emphasized how important it is to wrap expansions, such as `$myvar`, `${myvar[1]}`, and `${myvar##*/}`, in *double quotes*. Failing to do this *will* lead to bugs down the line when values contain characters that have special meaning to Bash, especially spaces. This is a common problem with code that has been cut and pasted from old documentation, or from bad advice posted on websites or in chat channels.

It only takes a few examples to realize how dangerous a failure to quote properly can be, *especially* in circumstances where files can be created by other users, and hence might include shell metacharacters. A file named `*`, for example, is *legal*, and if expanded incorrectly, can wreak havoc on your scripts:

```
$ cd ~/important
$ myfilename='*'
$ echo $myfilename
important-document  passwords-DO-NOT-DELETE  anniversary-plans
$ echo "$myfilename"
*
```

Imagine what might have happened if the first `echo` command here had been `rm` in a script instead!

In a few contexts in Bash, an expansion does not strictly require double quotes; none of these cases of `myvar` here require double quotes, due to their syntactic context:

```
newvar=$myvar
case $myvar in ...
[[ $myvar = "$othervar" ]]
```

However, adding double quotes in each of these cases does not do any harm, either:

```
newvar="$myvar"
case "$myvar" in ...
[[ "$myvar" = "$othervar" ]]
```

Similarly, watch for cases where you need more than one pair of nested quotes:

```
touch -- "$(basename -- "$filename")"
```

This might seem strange to those coming from other programming languages; it looks as if the two different sets of double quotes are mismatched. However, because one pair of quotes is inside a command substitution, the double quotes around it don't interfere with the expansion within it.

In summary, if you're in doubt about any given expansion: *quote it*!

You may occasionally run into objections of this sort: *I don't allow files with spaces or asterisks in their names on my system, so I don't need to quote.* Don't listen! Always use quoting to make your scripts safer and more robust.

When you don't want quotes

The previous section might have led you to ask, *What about if I actually do want the contents of my variable to undergo whitespace splitting and glob expansion?*

You may be tempted to do this to store a set of options for repeated use in later commands, for example:

```
# Not recommended
curlopts='--location --cookie-jar ~/cookies --cookie ~/cookies'
curl $curlopts --head -- http://www.example.org/
curl $curlopts -- http://www.example.net/
```

If we double-quoted the `$curlopts` expansions here, the options would be treated together as one argument, and wouldn't work correctly. However, this still seems to be a useful property of variables—so how can we use it safely?

The answer is that this is an ideal application of the **positional parameters** in the POSIX shell, or (preferably) **array variables** in Bash:

```
# POSIX (if necessary)
(
    set -- --location --cookie-jar ~/cookies --cookie ~/cookies
    curl "$@" --head -- http://www.example.org/
    curl "$@" -- http://www.example.net/
)
# Bash (better)
curlopts=(--location --cookie-jar ~/cookies --cookie ~/cookies)
curl "${curlopts[@]}" --head -- http://www.example.org/
curl "${curlopts[@]}" -- http://www.example.net/
```

The first form uses a **subshell**, surrounding the commands that require the `curl` options in parentheses, so that the `set` command that sets the positional parameters for reuse only applies within that block. This works, but it can be awkward to manage several such parameter stacks. If Bash is available, using arrays as in the second form makes the task much easier, and require such forced scoping.

You can build and store whole command strings this way, including the command name itself, executing it by simply expanding the whole array. Here's an example of building all the options and arguments for a `grep` command line:

```
#!/bin/bash

# Example starting values
extended=0
fixed=1
patterns=(foo bar)
extra_files=()
# Start with the grep command line
grepcmdline=(grep)
# If the extended or fixed flags are set, add -F or -E
if ((extended)) ; then
    grepcmdline+=(-E)
elif ((fixed)) ; then
    grepcmdline+=(-F)
fi
# Add each pattern to check
for pattern in "${patterns[@]}" ; do
    grepcmdline+=(-e "$pattern")
done
# Add option terminator
grepcmdline+=(--)
# Add files to check
grepcmdline+=(* "${extra_files[@]}")
# Run command!
"${grepcmdline[@]}"
```

This can be very useful for wrapper scripts, designed to simplify the use of a complicated command for one specific application, such as searching a fixed set of files for a set of patterns specified by the user.

Handling filenames starting with dashes

Recall that in any situation where a filename is stored in a variable, we must be careful when using it on a command line, because it might get interpreted as an option:

```
$ cp "$myvar" destdir
```

If `myvar` were a file named `-alphabet-`, this would result in a confusing error:

```
cp: invalid option -- 'h'
```

This is because the string was interpreted as a bundled set of options, and the letters a, l, and p are all valid options for the GNU cp command, but h is not.

We can address this one of two main ways; the first, for the commands that support it, is to use the -- terminator string option:

```
$ cp -- "$myvar" destdir
```

This signals to the cp command that every word after that argument is *not* an option, but (in this case) a file or directory name to operate on.

Unfortunately, while this is a very widespread convention, not every command supports these terminators. For such commands, a more general way to make this work is to specify the path in a form that *doesn't* start with a dash, whether by fully qualifying it from the filesystem root, or just by prefixing it with ./:

```
$ myscript /home/bashuser/-alphabet
$ myscript ./-alphabet
```

This also works fine in loops:

```
cd data || exit
for file in * ; do
    myscript ./"$file"
done
```

Separating output and diagnostics

Remember always to write error output from your script to the standard error file descriptor, not to output, using the >&2 redirection:

```
#!/bin/bash
if ! [[ -e $myfile ]] ; then
    printf >&2 '%s does not exist!\n' "$myfile"
    exit 1
fi
```

This allows users to redirect any output the script generates separately from the errors. This applies to non-fatal warnings or diagnostic information just as much as to error messages.

Keeping scripts brief and simple

The ideal shell script is a relatively *short* one, because shell script has such limited support for concepts such as variable scope, no support for a library or module system for robust packaging, a lot of global state of various kinds, and very limited data typing.

Instead of trying to write one very long program that does many things, follow the Unix tradition of writing shorter, smaller programs that do one thing each, and that do that thing very well.

If you find your Bash program is becoming too large and unwieldy, and you can't simplify it, consider translating it to Perl, Python, or a similar general-purpose program instead. This is quite normal; shell script has been used since its earliest days as a **prototyping language**, in exactly this way.

Keeping scripts flexible

Allow your script's users to use the tool in whatever way they may need. For example, avoid hardcoding filenames to be read in your scripts, if you can; instead, allow the user to provide filenames as options or arguments.

If your script works on files, consider making it work the same way the classic Unix text filtering tools do. If there are no arguments, read any data needed from the standard input:

```
$ myscript
```

If there *are* arguments, read the data from (or make changes to) all of those files, in order:

```
$ myscript file1 file2
```

If one of the arguments is a dash, read from the standard input at that point in the argument loop, to allow us to provide a prefix and a suffix to the data:

```
$ myscript file1 - file2
```

These conventions are well-known to Unix users, and they will appreciate finding this flexibility in your scripts.

Respecting and applying the user's configuration

Never assume a user's choice of line-text editor ($EDITOR), visual-text editor ($VISUAL), shell ($SHELL), or web browser ($BROWSER). Instead, fall back to sensible defaults if these values are *not* set, using the :- form of parameter expansion:

```
#!/bin/bash
read -p 'Now editing your configuration file (press ENTER): '
"${VISUAL:-vi}" -- "$HOME"/.myscriptrc
```

The preceding script will wait for an *Enter* key press (well, a line entry, technically). It then starts the user's choice of visual-text editor if it's set, or defaults to vi if it's not, which should be installed on most Unix-like systems. In some circumstances, such as a script for use by beginners, a more sensible default choice might be nano. Consider carefully what your script's users might *expect* to happen; avoid giving them any nasty surprises.

Choose to invoke VISUAL instead of EDITOR to start an editor for interactive scripts; it is much more likely to present the user with an editor they can use.

Allowing scripts to run without user input

If your script requires user data during its run in order to make decisions on what to do, it can be tempting to prompt the user for each required bit of information when needed, perhaps using the -p option to the read builtin to request a prompt:

```
#!/bin/bash
read -p 'Do you want to create the directory? [y/N]: ' createdir
case $createdir in
    y*|Y*)
        mkdir -- "$HOME"/myscript || exit
        ;;
esac
```

This example will only create the directory named in the `dir` variable if a string such as `y` or `YES` (or `yoyo`!) is read from standard input, and assumes that it is likely to be the user's terminal.

This is convenient for interactive scripts, but it assumes that the user running the script is actually at a terminal, and it makes the script awkward to use in automation; someone trying to call this script automatically from `cron` or `systemd` would need to arrange to pipe in a single line, `yes`, to make it work. If the script needs to read from a data file at some point, it also complicates passing further data into it via the standard input.

If you need to make whether to do something during the script's run configurable, consider using a command-line option instead:

```
case $1 in
    -c|--createdir)
        mkdir -- "$HOME"/myscript || exit
        shift
        ;;
esac
```

Now the need for the behavior can be specified on the command line:

```
$ myscript -c
$ myscript --createdir
```

In some cases, it can even be desirable to put the variable in a configuration file, to be read at startup from a known path:

```
#!/bin/bash
if [[ -r $HOME/.myscriptrc ]] ; then
    source "$HOME"/.myscriptrc
fi
case $createdir in
    y*|Y*)
        mkdir -- "$HOME"/myscript || exit
        ;;
esac
```

The preceding script uses `source` to run all of the Bash commands in the `~/.myscriptrc` file, if it exists. If this configuration file contains a definition of `createdir` as anything starting with `y` or `Y`, the directory will be created:

```
$ cat ~/.myscriptrc
createdir=yes
```

If, for whatever reason, your script really does need user input, which sometimes happens in secure contexts where you need to read straight from the terminal device, consider including an optional mode named `--batch`, `--force`, or a similar name that proceeds without that input, skipping all the prompts by assuming a sensible default for an answer:

```bash
#!/bin/bash
case $1 in
    -b|--batch)
        batch=1
        shift
        ;;
esac
if ((batch)) ; then
    createdir=y
else
    read -p 'Do you want to create the directory? [y/N]: ' createdir
fi
case $createdir in
    y*|Y*)
        mkdir -- "$HOME"/myscript || exit
        ;;
esac
```

Limiting the scope of shell state changes

If you are going to change properties of the shell as a whole in part of your script, consider limiting the scope of that change only to the needed part of the script to avoid unexpected effects on the rest of it. Watch for these in particular:

- The working directory
- The positional parameters ($1, $2 ...)
- Environment variables, especially PATH
- Shell-local variables, especially IFS
- Shell options with set (such as -x) or shopt (such as dotglob)
- Shell resource limits set with ulimit

We already saw one effective means of limiting the scope of *variables* in Chapter 5, *Variables and Patterns*, by applying them as prefixes to a command:

```
IFS=: read -r name address
```

This limits the scope of the IFS change to the read command only.

For other types of shell state change, we have to get a bit more creative:

- Keeping the script itself so short that the change doesn't matter
- Changing the state back to its original value again as soon as possible
- Making the change in a subshell so that it doesn't affect the rest of the program
- Rewriting to avoid the change entirely

The last option is by far the most desirable; if the command itself can do what you need, don't reinvent that wheel in Bash!

Here is an example based on a common problem: the following script changes into the working directory of a Git repository in ~/src/bash, and fetches any changes from its default remote branch:

```
cd -- "$HOME"/src/bash || exit
git fetch
```

The problem is that the script needs to change its directory to do this, and then needs to change *back* to whatever directory it started in before proceeding with the rest of the script.

We could do this manually by saving the current working directory in a variable named pwd before changing it to the repository directory, and then changing back to the saved path after we are done:

```
pwd=$PWD
cd -- "$HOME"/src/bash || exit
git fetch
cd -- "$pwd" || exit
```

We could make the change in a subshell, so that it does not change the state of the surrounding script; this is complicated, however, as we then need to add an extra exit to catch a failure to change directory at all, and || true to ignore error conditions from git fetch, since that's what the original does:

```
(
    cd -- "$HOME"/src/bash || exit
    git fetch || true
) || exit
```

The best method in this case is to use the git program's -C option to specify the working directory for the command, allowing us to reduce this to just one line:

```
git -C "$HOME"/src/bash fetch
```

If you apply a little care to managing global state like this, your scripts will be much easier to edit later.

Avoiding path anti-patterns

Some shell script programmers use absolute paths for even common system tools:

```
/bin/sed '/^$/d' data
```

This command line is intended to print the contents of the data file, but to skip blank lines. It does work on most GNU/Linux systems, but why specify the full /bin/sed path? Why not just sed?

Worse, sometimes people try to abbreviate this by saving the full paths in variables, after retrieving them with a non-standard tool such as which:

```
# Terrible code; never do this!
SED=$(which sed)
$SED '/^$d/' data
```

 Can you see anything else wrong with this code? Hint: what was the very first thing we re-emphasized in this chapter?

This use of which and full paths such as this is unnecessary, and there are no advantages to doing it. Bash will already search PATH for you for any command name; you don't need to rely on which (or even type -P) to do it for you.

Besides being unnecessarily verbose, there are other problems with this approach; this script isn't *respectful*, because it doesn't apply the user's choice of $PATH, and worse, it's not *portable*: on some Unix systems, the sed program may not be in /bin, but in /usr/bin, or even something very hard to predict, such as /usr/xpg4/bin (yes, really!).

So, keep it simple; just call sed, and let the system figure the rest of it out:

```
sed '/^$/d' data
```

Avoiding Bash for untrusted user input

Shell script is not a language that was designed with the security of untrusted input in mind, and because shell scripting interpreters are generally used for situations in which a user is at least partly already trusted to run processes on the box, they do not heavily prioritize security or security audits.

When you give a user a system shell account on your server, even if you don't give them root privileges, you are trusting them to some extent not to abuse the system or damage it. Executing code using the same tools from someone on the internet that you *don't* trust is a recipe for disaster!

Highly publicized vulnerabilities, such as 2014's "ShellShock," resulted largely from abuse of the Bash shell as part of generating responses to requests from the internet. Bash is a system-command interpreter, and was never designed to be used in this way – it was created years before the World Wide Web even existed. It takes significant effort and expertise to make a task using shell scripting languages safe to run with data from the web; there are just too many ways to allow arbitrary code-execution in the language.

Therefore, at least until you are a shell script expert and familiar with all of these dark corners, don't attempt to sanitize untrusted data from the internet with Bash. Your author has studied shell scripting for many years, and still wouldn't do it. Use a web-based programming language instead, where security – while never perfect – is both important and emphasized, and frequently reviewed. PHP or Python are both good starting points.

 If you're writing scripts that parse trusted web pages using a tool such as curl, always make requests from an HTTPS version of the site, and resist the temptation to turn off certificate verification – it's there to protect you!

Documenting scripts

Just as with any kind of programming, it's important to write some documentation to help your users understand and run your program, and to know all of its available features. We'll look at three documentation methods: writing **comments**, providing **help output**, and writing **manual pages**.

Writing comments

It's good practice to add comments to any code to explain what it's doing to the curious (or debugging) reader, and Bash is no exception. Keep your comments concise, up-to-date, and most of all, useful. Remember: don't just rephrase what the code is doing; explain *why* you're doing it, not just *what* it does.

Consider this comment and line of shell script:

```
# Loop to end of positional params
for targetdir ; do : ; done
```

Is the comment here helpful to someone reading the script? Can you tell what the code is doing? Consider the following comment instead, which explains the *purpose* of the unclear code, even to a user who may not do much shell programming:

```
# Save last command line argument as target directory
for targetdir ; do : ; done
```

That's much better.

Providing help output

Consider providing a little help to users of your script if they try running it with a -h or --help option; even a single line showing which arguments are expected and in what order can be very helpful:

```
case $1 in
    -h|--help)
        printf 'USAGE: myscript [--verbose] FILE1 [FILE2...] TARGETDIR\n'
        ;;
esac
```

The manual page describing manual pages on GNU/Linux systems, viewable with man man-pages, gives some information on common expected formats for these usage strings.

Writing manual pages

To really do your scripts' users a service, consider writing a fully-fledged manual page for the man reader tool, in a format such as mandoc: https://mandoc.bsd.lv/.

In addition to trying `myscript -h` or `myscript --help`, many users will try `man myscript` in their search for help. Why not impress them with a full page of readily-available documentation, showing a detailed explanation of what the tool is for, some usage instructions, and even some examples? You can even convert the manual page to be published on the web using `mandoc`, for those users more inclined to use the web to search for answers to a problem.

 Don't underestimate the importance of writing comments, help, and documentation even just for *yourself* in the future – it's very easy to forget how even your own code works. Writing about your code also helps you to think more clearly about its design, and what it should (and should not) do.

Using temporary files cleanly

If you need a temporary file in your script to store data for the script's run, it can be tempting to assume a fixed path for the file in `/tmp`:

```
# Store the current date for later
# Requires GNU/BSD `date` with non-POSIX %s format
date +%s > /tmp/myscript-timestamp
```

`/tmp` exists on virtually all Unix systems, which makes it a popular choice. However, this approach has some risks:

- There may be a safer or more suitable location for temporary files specified by the system, or preferred by the user, such as `/var/tmp`. The `/tmp` directory might be very strictly locked down in some environments, especially PCI-DSS-compliant systems.
- If the temporary filename name is not unique, and more than one instance of the script runs at once, the behavior can be unpredictable and hard to debug.
- Because `/tmp` is world-writable, if an attacker can write to and predict the name of the data file in `/tmp`, they could edit it before the script finishes, possibly hijacking the script.

The name of the temporary directory is often available in the `TMPDIR` environment variable, which can improve this approach a little, while still using `/tmp` as a fallback:

```
date +%s > "${TMPDIR:-/tmp}"/myscript-timestamp
```

However, perhaps the best approach is the use of the mktemp tool, if it's available. It creates temporary files or directories, and prints the name of whatever it created. It should do this creation relatively safely, with a randomized name, and in a location and pattern that's consistent with the system's settings:

```
$ mktemp -d
/tmp/tmp.mmfGKhMxtv
```

We can use this to safely pick a temporary directory for our script each run:

```
tempdir=$(mktemp -d) || exit
date +%s > "$tempdir"/myscript-timestamp
```

Note that we abort the script if the temporary directory could not be created; || exit runs only if the mktemp command in the variable assignment fails.

mktemp is not a standard POSIX tool, so it's not guaranteed to be available, but it's very common on many Unix-like systems, including Linux and BSD. Use it if you can.

Cleaning up after a script

Dropping temporary files without cleaning them up is a little untidy; at the end of a script where temporary files are used, we should have a safe rm command to remove them afterward:

```
#!/bin/bash

# Code setting and using tempdir goes here, and then ...

# Remove the directory
if [[ -n $tempdir ]] ; then
    rm -- "$tempdir"/myscript-timestamp
    rmdir -- "$tempdir"
fi
```

Notice that we're careful to check that tempdir actually has a value, using the -n test before we run this code, even if we don't think anything might have changed it; otherwise we'd be running rm -- /myscript-timestamp.

Notice also that we're carefully removing only the files we know we've created, rather than just specifying "$tempdir"/*. An empty value for the tempdir variable in such a case could have terrible consequences!

The preceding code is a good start for the ending of a script – but what about cases where a script is interrupted? Ideally, we'd delete the files even if someone pressed *Ctrl + C* to interrupt the script before it was finished.

Bash provides an EXIT **trap** for this purpose; we can define a command that should be run whenever the script exits, if it can possibly run it. The very start of our Bash script might look like this:

```
cleanup() {
    if [[ -n $tempdir ]] ; then
        rm -f -- "$tempdir"/myscript-timestamp
        rmdir -f -- "$tempdir"
    fi
}
trap cleanup EXIT
tempdir=$(mktemp -d) || exit
```

The cleanup function is run whenever the Bash script exits, and hasn't been sent the SIGKILL or kill -9 signal. If the tempdir variable is set, it tries to clear away a temporary file in it, and then remove the temporary directory itself. Notice that we set up the hook *first*, before the temporary directory is even created, to get it in place as soon as possible.

> If this boilerplate code bothers you, see whether you can write your script without using temporary files. Compound commands and creative use of pipes can help a lot here.

Tools to check shell scripts for problems

The ShellCheck tool is a **linter** for shell script, designed to find bugs and trouble spots in various flavors of shell scripts, including Bash. It identifies many of the common errors discussed in this book, and many more besides. It is available as both an online service and a command-line tool at https://www.shellcheck.net/.

The output of ShellCheck points you directly to trouble spots in your code, including error codes for reference with its online documentation:

```
~$ shellcheck wro.bash

In wro.bash line 13:
if [ -n $1 ] ; then
         ^-- SC2070: -n doesn't work with unquoted arguments. Quote or use [[ ]].
         ^-- SC2086: Double quote to prevent globbing and word splitting.
```

Summary

We've gone over some of the most important techniques in good use of Bash shell script, with particular emphasis on keeping things small, simple, and robust. With all we've learned, however, we've still only just scratched the surface.

As we mentioned in the first few chapters, because Bash is largely designed to run other programs and make them work together—sometimes in novel ways the authors of those programs could never have imagined—we could fill a book this size many times over just with various tips and tricks for elegant shell script programming for many of our favourite commands.

We hope that this short book has given you a running start in becoming an expert shell script user, and helped you begin to appreciate the power and flexibility that knowledgeable use of the Bash shell offers you. Your author believes that mastering some form of command shell is one of the best decisions a programmer or systems administrator can make, and Bash is a great choice. It provides amazing possibilities for writing powerful programs very quickly in only a few lines, and automating boring or error-prone jobs to make your work more productive, satisfying, challenging, and—maybe best of all—more fun.

Other Books You May Enjoy

If you enjoyed this book, you may be interested in these other books by Packt:

Penetration Testing with the Bash shell
Keith Makan

ISBN: 978-1-84969-510-7

- Perform network enumeration techniques with Dig, whois, dnsenum, dnsmap, and others
- Learn how to fuzz and reverse engineer using the Kali Linux command line tools
- Exploit common web application vulnerabilities using skipfish, arcachi, and sqlmap
- Accomplish man-in-the-middle attacks straight from your command line
- Assess SSL security using sslyze and openssl
- Carry out network traffic analysis using tcpdump

Bash Cookbook
Ron Brash, Ganesh Naik

ISBN: 978-1-78862-936-2

- Understand the basics of Bash shell scripting on a Linux system
- Gain working knowledge of how redirections and pipes interact
- Retrieve and parse input or output of any command
- Automate tasks such as data collection and creating and applying a patch
- Create a script that acts like a program with different features
- Customize your Bash shell and discover neat tricks to extend your programs
- Compile and install shell and log commands on your system's console using Syslog

Leave a review - let other readers know what you think

Please share your thoughts on this book with others by leaving a review on the site that you bought it from. If you purchased the book from Amazon, please leave us an honest review on this book's Amazon page. This is vital so that other potential readers can see and use your unbiased opinion to make purchasing decisions, we can understand what our customers think about our products, and our authors can see your feedback on the title that they have worked with Packt to create. It will only take a few minutes of your time, but is valuable to other potential customers, our authors, and Packt. Thank you!

Index

E

environment variables 84
errors
  blocking 65
  combining, with output 64
  output, sending 66
  redirecting 63
executable bit 139
exit values 25, 133

F

filenames
  handling, with dashes 150
find command
  executing 51
  xargs 52
fixed arithmetic 94
floating-point arithmetic 93
forked process 83
functions
  about 129
  arguments, obtaining 132
  arguments, passing 130
  defining 129
  input and output 134
  options, separating from filenames 131
  reloading, at shell startup 137
  scope 135
  used, in script 145
  values, returning 133
  versus script 144

G

globs
  case-insensitive globbing 98
  configuring 96
  dot and dot-dot file, excluding 96
  dot files, including 96
  expanding 97
  extended globbing 98
  using 94
group command 74

H

hash-bang 139
here-document 69

I

if keyword
  [command, using 106
  [[keyword, using 106
  arithmetic conditions 107
  test command, using 105
  using 103
infinite loop 116
input redirection 67
input
  long string, used with here-documents 69
  redirecting 67
integers 108
interactive key bindings 20
interpreter 139
ls command
  filename lists, obtaining 41
iteration 110

L

lexicographic tests 108
linter 162
locale settings 86
logical binary directories (bindirs) 141
loops 103

M

metacharacters 21

O

option terminator 131
output
  created file permissions 60
  created files, permissions selecting 62
  files, appending 60
  overwrites, avoiding 59
  redirecting 57
  redirection paths 58
  separating 151

Made in the USA
Monee, IL
14 December 2021

85483298R00103